BEACH HUT

LIGHTHOUSE

BATHYSPHERE

SUNSHINE

MARTIN JOHNSON'S
amazing
MARITIME
MODELS

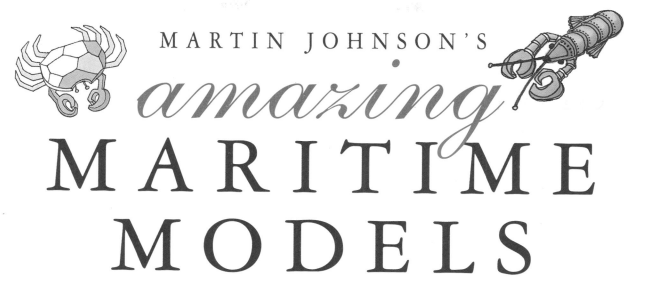

MARTIN JOHNSON'S
amazing
MARITIME
MODELS

GLASS

THIN CHAIN

David & Charles

A DAVID & CHARLES BOOK
Copyright © Martin Johnson 1995
First Published 1995

Photography Paul Biddle

Martin Johnson has asserted his right to be identified as author of this
work in accordance with the Copyright, Designs and Patents Act 1988.

A catalogue record of this book is available from the British Library.

ISBN 0 7153 0186 1

Printed in Italy by LEGO SpA
for David & Charles
Brunel House Newton Abbot Devon

CONTENTS

'BIRDS EYE'

INTRODUCTION

The theme of the projects in this book is always the same – life above and below the water. Most are combinations of boats, fish, water and the sea bed and offer a glimpse of the working life of the sea.

While working on new projects, I follow more or less the same system each time. When I have an idea I commit it to paper as a rough sketch as soon as possible – a visual note that can be developed or discarded at a later date. I find that my first drawing is often the best so I keep all sketches until I have worked the idea into something a little more definite. You can see from the 'Bird's Eye' examples here that there is a remarkable similarity between my initial drawing and the finished result.

Once the idea is on paper I begin the painstaking and fairly complicated process of turning it into a thing of substance. My experience of construction has taught me to keep instructions simple and minimal, this applies equally to building a 60-foot galleon for Captain Birdseye as it does to making a small-scale model. The instructions in this book are no different. They are brief and straightforward and you should be able to make all the models simply by following the diagrams and the step-by-step notes.

Each model is shown in stages from the first sketch through working drawings to the finished scene.

Throughout the book there are pages of 'ideas' – identifiable by their red borders. These show preliminary sketches of scenes other than those in the ten projects. These drawings are visual notes, from which you may find some inspiration for future models of your own. Some of my rough ideas can become quite abstract. *Sunshine* (page 23), for example, was an attempt to portray the effect of sunlight passing through water. Others are simpler in intent – such as *Lighthouse* (page 23), which aims to offer a secret glimpse of life inside a working lighthouse.

'BIRDS EYE'
ON THE TOWN

TOOLS
& MATERIALS

－ － － － － －

TOOLS

There are a only a few tools needed for the projects in this book. They are described below.

I use a Dewalt DW 100 bandsaw, which allows timber to be cut to all the sizes and thicknesses required for the projects in this book. It also enables gentle curves to be cut in timber up to 2in (50mm) in thickness. Black & Decker's BD 339 bandsaw is also suitable. If no bandsaw is available a hand coping saw can be used.

One of the advantages of the Dewalt bandsaw is that it has a 6in (15cm) disc sander built on to the side. This is useful to sand facets and generally clean up the timber. I find disc sanders better than either belt or orbital sanders. A disc sander attached to any power drill would also be fine. A set of small files is also very handy for cleaning up any difficult corners.

The next most important tool is a fretsaw. I use a Vibro 2000 Aereopiccola which is marvellous as it produces a smooth saw cut,

considerably reducing cleaning up. The Proxxon DSH 2 fretsaw is also suitable. A hand fretsaw can also be used.

A drill is necessary – either hand or power. The most useful one is a stand drill with a chuck capable of taking a drill up to 1/2in (12mm) diameter. The stand allows very thin needle drills to be used without danger of breaking and helps to ensure accurate perpendicular or angled holes. An ordinary power drill on a stand would suffice.

In some projects it is helpful to have access to a lathe. I use a Record DML 24 lathe which is plenty powerful enough for small work. Alternatively you can buy a lathe kit to fit most hand held electric drills. It is worth noting that most evening classes in woodwork have access to a lathe.

A small router is required to form the moulded edge to the top and base of the glass cases (see page 49).

The symbols overleaf each stand for a different tool. The diagrams in each project make it clear which tool is used for each job.

MATERIALS

The first project *Fishing Boat at Sea* (page 12) has a detailed list of the materials needed. Use this as a guide to what is required for the other projects.

Very small quantities of softwood are required. It is unnecessary to have many different thicknesses as all items can be cut from pieces of 3 x 1in (80 x 25mm) wood. The various dowels and plys are all readily available from any model shop. Buy a few items each time you visit and you will quickly build up a good stock from which subsequent models can be constructed.

Other items you will need are hardboard, medium density fibreboard (MDF), wooden beads, piano wire, aluminium mesh, brass wire and nails, plastic map pins, copper tubing and a selection of sandpapers. These are easily obtained from model shops.

GLUING AND STICKING

Any fast (and clear) drying white wood adhesive is ideal and it is easily cleaned up as it dries. Cellulose car body filler is used to set the boats into the waves and can be teased into foaming wave shapes as it hardens. It is also used to fix items to glass.

PAINT AND VARNISH

Acrylic paint is the best paint to use as it can be thinned with water to be used as a wash if required, but is opaque and quick-drying when used undiluted. It may be necessary to sand between coats of paint as water tends to raise the grain of the wood. It is often better to paint items before gluing them together. When the paint is dry apply several coats of gloss varnish.

GLASS AND GLASS CASES

Glass can be obtained from any good glazier, who will be quite happy to cut it to shape and size as required. You will need clear glass for the glass case and Flemish glass for the surface of the water. See page 49 for details on making the glass cases.

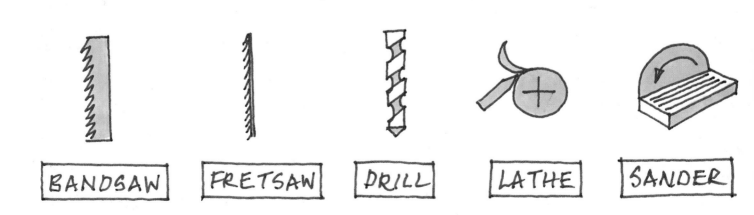

BANDSAW   FRETSAW   DRILL   LATHE   SANDER

FISHING BOAT
at Sea

Caught in a rough sea, this small fishing boat is a stylized version of the type of inshore craft to be seen all around the coast. The object is to create the impression of a boat at sea rather than making an accurate reproduction with slavish attention to detail. Extreme liberties have been taken with the scale of various elements to accentuate the event, rather like a cartoon. Despite the boat's predicament, the feeling is of fun rather than menace.

DRILL WOODEN BEADS

2

JAN

DOWEL

Guidelines for buying materials are on page 10 and amounts are given on page 16. All plans, elevations and templates are drawn to full size so that they can be traced directly off the page. Read through the instructions before starting and gather together all the materials you need. Remember it is easier to paint items before gluing them together. This model does not have a glass case.

DIMENSIONS OF THE MODEL

depth 5in (13cm), width 7³/₄in (20cm),
height 5¹/₂in (14cm).

FISH

1 Using the 2 x 1in (50 x 25mm) timber on edge, cut the waves. Try to feel their sway on the bandsaw. Make them vary in depth, some thick and others thin. The exposed grain sometimes makes very interesting patterns, which can add to the watery effect.

2 Clean the cut timber with sandpaper then glue it to a baseboard of either hardboard or plywood.

3 Cut the hull of the boat from 3 x 1in (75 x 25mm) timber using the full-size plan (page 19) as a template. Cut out the inner shape with a fretsaw as shown in the diagram page 17. Push it out and cut it crossways so that you have two identical pieces of half the depth. Glue one piece back in place.

4 Use the hull as a template to mark the boat's position in the waves. Cut out the shape.

5 Cut out all the elements of the boat – the wheelhouse, lifebuoy, engine box, hatch and lights. These are quite straightforward to make from pieces of wood, ply and dowel; the full-size section and plan illustrate the dimensions. Paint the items before gluing them together.

6 Cut the fish from scraps of wood as shown (page 21), and make the surface facets by sanding.

7 Make the marker buoy with a section of 1in (25mm) dowel sanded into a cone. Drill a piece of ¹/₈in (3mm) dowel into the top and thread a wooden bead on to it.

8 The masts and boom are made from dowel and beads, the sail from ¹/₁₆in (1.6mm) plywood.

9 The fisherman is made from a combination of various sizes of dowel and has a wooden bead for his head.

10 The fishing net is a piece of aluminium mesh with wooden beads, cut half way through, glued to its edges.

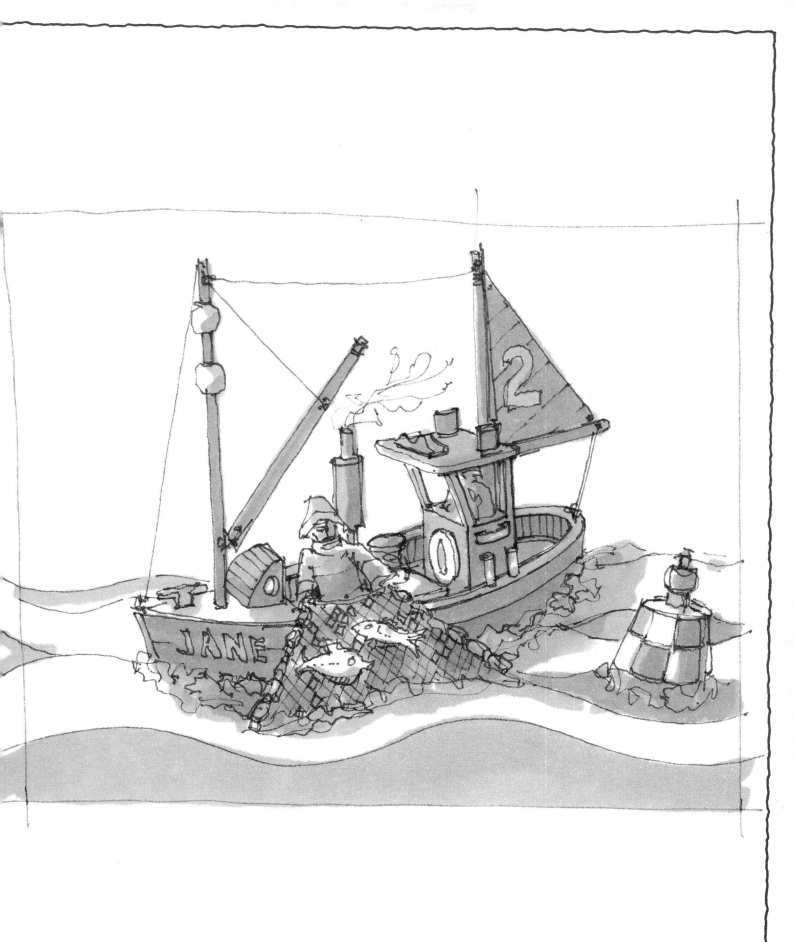

MATERIALS LIST

	Size		Length	
Timber	3x1in	(75x25mm)	6in	(150mm)
Timber	2x1in	(50x25mm)	36in	(900mm)
Dowel	$\frac{1}{16}$in	(1.6mm)	6in	(150mm)
Dowel	$\frac{1}{8}$in	(3mm)	18in	(450mm)
Dowel	$\frac{3}{8}$in	(10mm)	6in	(150mm)
Dowel	$\frac{1}{2}$in	(12mm)	6in	(150mm)
Hardboard	$\frac{1}{4}$in	(6mm)	12x6in	(300x150mm)
Plywood	$\frac{1}{16}$in	(1.6in)	3x3in	(75x75mm)
Brass wire	$\frac{1}{32}$in	(1mm)	12in	(300mm)
Wooden beads	$\frac{1}{4}$in	(6mm)	12 required	

• White wood adhesive • Cellulose car body filler
• Flemish glass • Aluminium mesh • Acrylic paint • Gloss varnish

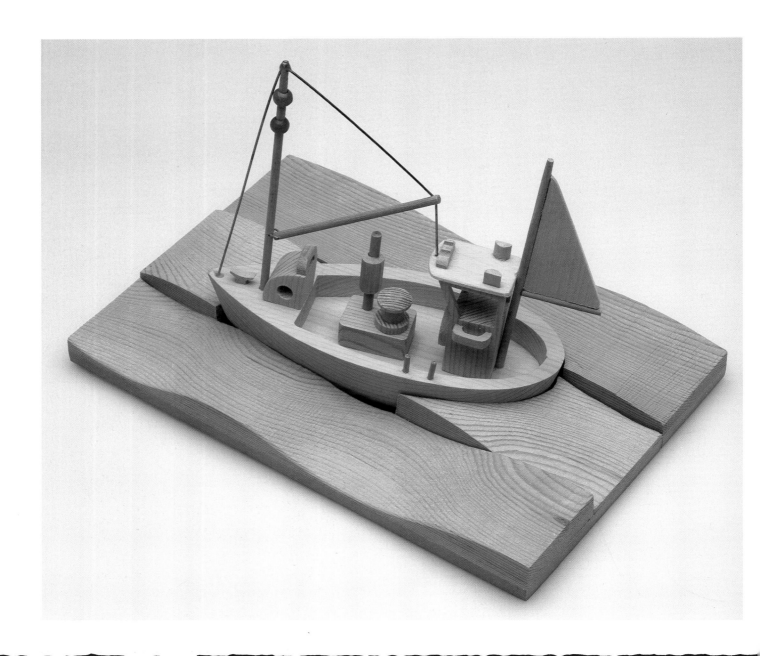

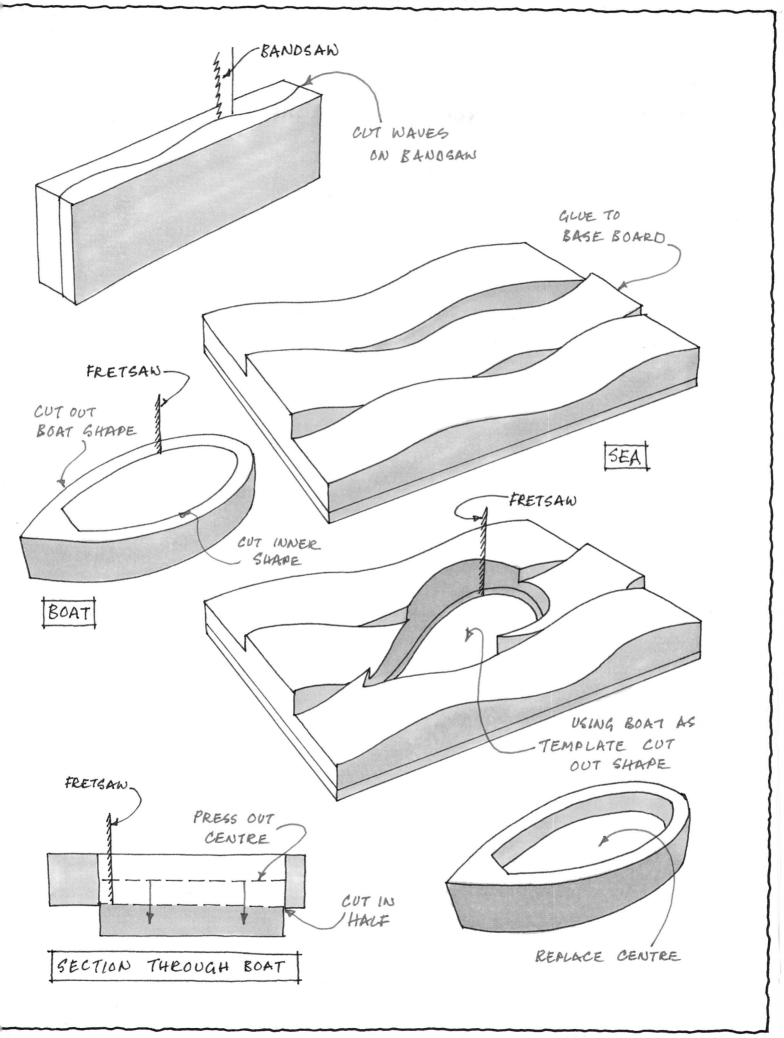

BANDSAW

CUT WAVES
ON BANDSAW

GLUE TO
BASE BOARD

SEA

FRETSAW

CUT OUT
BOAT SHAPE

CUT INNER
SHAPE

BOAT

FRETSAW

USING BOAT AS
TEMPLATE CUT
OUT SHAPE

FRETSAW

PRESS OUT
CENTRE

CUT IN
HALF

SECTION THROUGH BOAT

REPLACE CENTRE

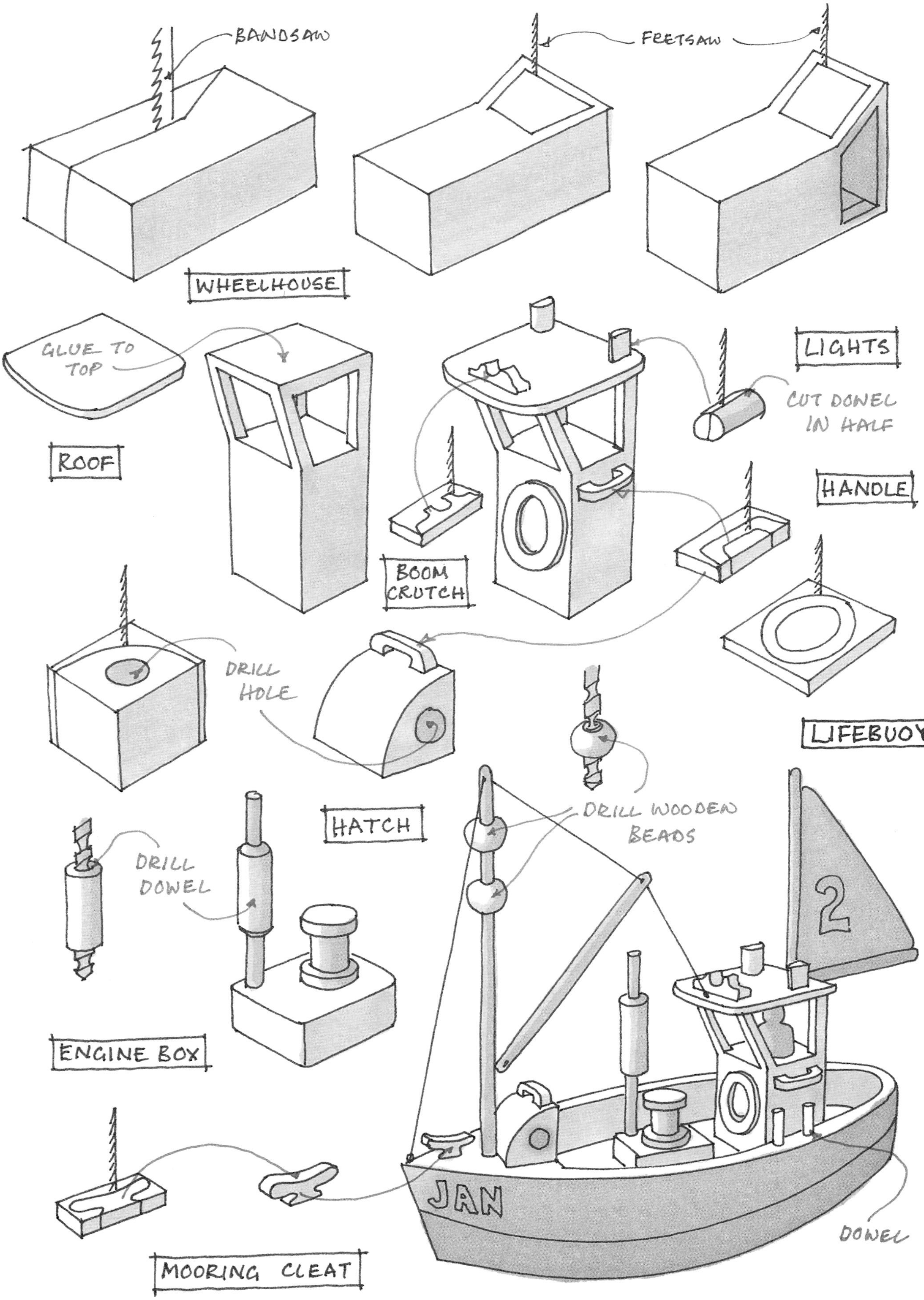

BANDSAW

FRETSAW

WHEELHOUSE

GLUE TO TOP

ROOF

LIGHTS

CUT DOWEL IN HALF

HANDLE

BOOM CRUTCH

DRILL HOLE

LIFEBUOY

HATCH

DRILL WOODEN BEADS

DRILL DOWEL

ENGINE BOX

2

JAN

DOWEL

MOORING CLEAT

THE BOAT

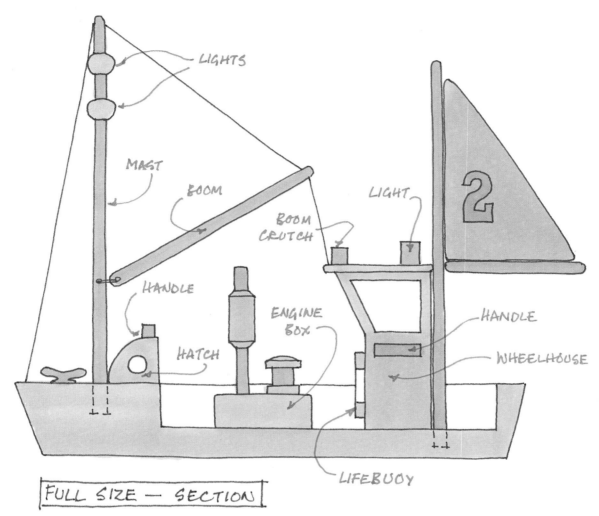

LIGHTS

MAST

BOOM

BOOM CRUTCH

LIGHT

HANDLE

HATCH

ENGINE BOX

HANDLE

WHEELHOUSE

LIFEBUOY

2

FULL SIZE — SECTION

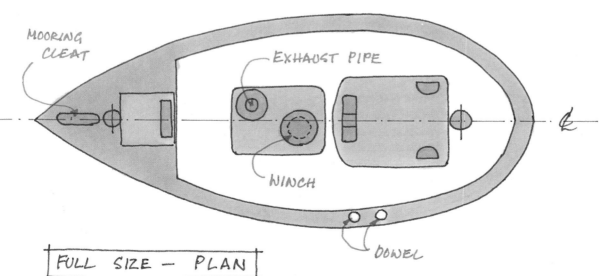

MOORING CLEAT

EXHAUST PIPE

WINCH

DOWEL

FULL SIZE — PLAN

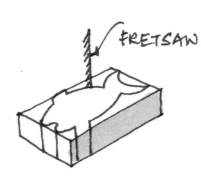
FRETSAW

SAND FACETS

SANDER

FISH

BRASS WIRE

CUT WOODEN BEADS

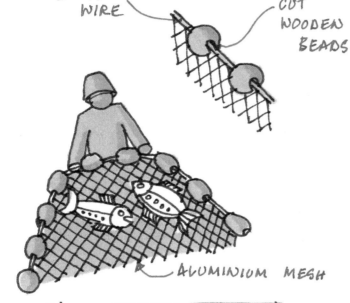
ALUMINIUM MESH

FISHERMAN + NET

WOODEN BEAD

THIN DOWEL

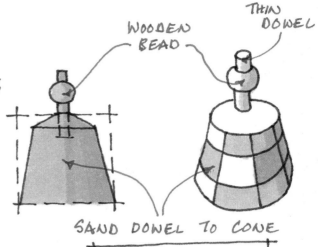
SAND DOWEL TO CONE

MARKER BUOY

WOODEN BEAD HEAD

DOWEL

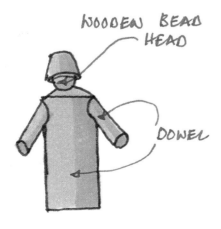

FISHERMAN

FISH

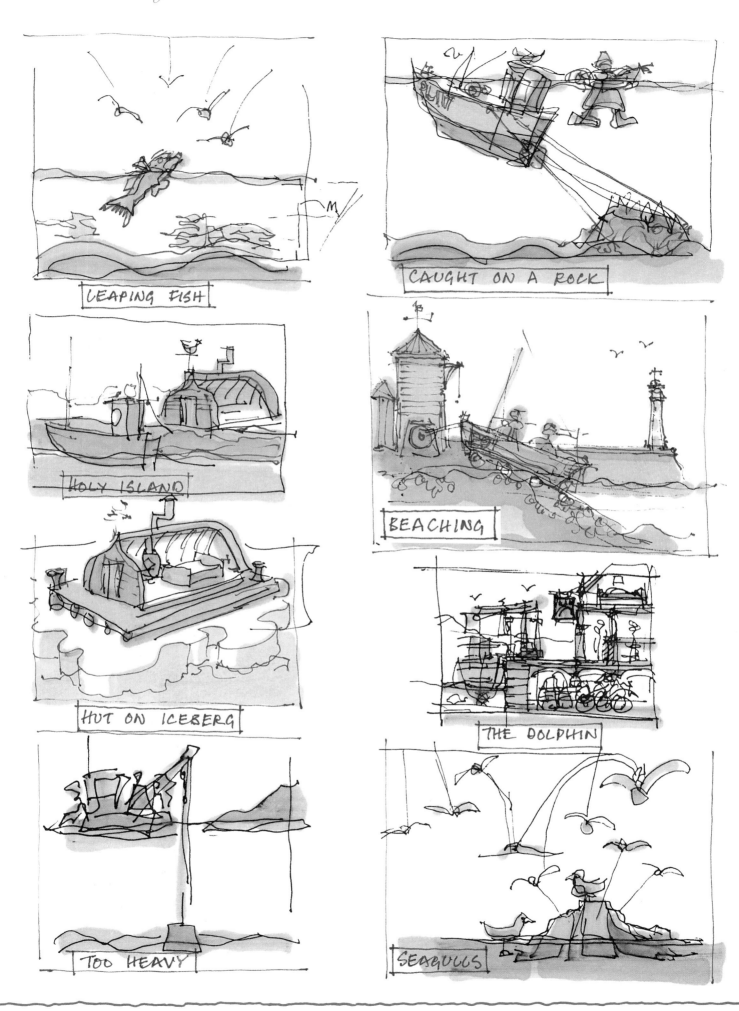

LEAPING FISH

CAUGHT ON A ROCK

HOLY ISLAND

BEACHING

HUT ON ICEBERG

THE DOLPHIN

TOO HEAVY

SEAGULLS

BEACH HUT

LIGHTHOUSE

BATHYSPHERE

SUNSHINE

a long day's FISHING

- - - - - - -

A light-hearted look at life above and below the sea, this scene explores the magic of being able to see both situations at the same time. The design uses a decorative back board thus producing a vertical dimension. Above the surface of the sea is a wooden landscape with lighthouse, below is an underwater rock formation. On the water is a rock with a fishing rod and a seagull on it.

Guidelines for buying materials are given on page 10. All plans, elevations and templates are drawn to full size so that they can be traced directly off the page. Read through the instructions before starting and gather together all the materials you need.
Remember it is easier to paint items before gluing them together. This model does not have a glass case.

DIMENSIONS OF THE MODEL
depth 4in (10cm), width 4³/₄in (12cm),
height 12¹/₂in (31cm).

1 The back board is a piece of ¹/₂in (12mm) MDF. Using a saw, cut a groove half way up and half way through its thickness. This will accommodate the glass, which is the surface of the water. Cut the top of the back board to form clouds above the horizon. Below the horizon cut curving chunks out of sides of the back board using a fretsaw echoing wave formations.

2 Make the sea bed in the same way as the waves in *Fishing Boat at Sea* (page 17). Cut curves into the edges of the wood, making more complex shapes. Glue this to the back board.

3 The surface of the sea is a curved section of Flemish glass cut to shape and the edge polished (a glazier will be happy to do this). It is attached to the back board with cellulose car body filler.

4 Use pieces of timber to make the rock formation in much the same way as the sea bed, stick it to the glass with cellulose car body filler.

5 Make the fishing rod and line from a length of brass wire with some sections of dowel threaded on for the reel and handle as shown in the diagram. Glue them in place. The rod stand is also made from wire, bend it to shape and drill a hole in the rock to sit it in. Attach the line to the end of the rod and, at the surface of the water, cut the wire and glue it to the glass with half a bead. Glue the other half directly below it on the underside of the glass. Use cellulose car body filler for this and make small, watery ripples on the surface as it sets. Attach a bead at the end of the wire, bending the last section into a hook shape.

6 Make the lighthouse by turning a piece of ¹/₄in (6mm) dowel on a lathe. Cut out the landscape. Paint both, then attach them to the glass with cellulose car body filler.

7 The seaweed, bird, crab and fish are made with skin ply and scraps of timber following the diagrams in this chapter. Sand the facets and then paint. Drill a thin piece of piano wire into the back of each fish to attach it to the back board. Stick the seaweed and crab to the sea bed.

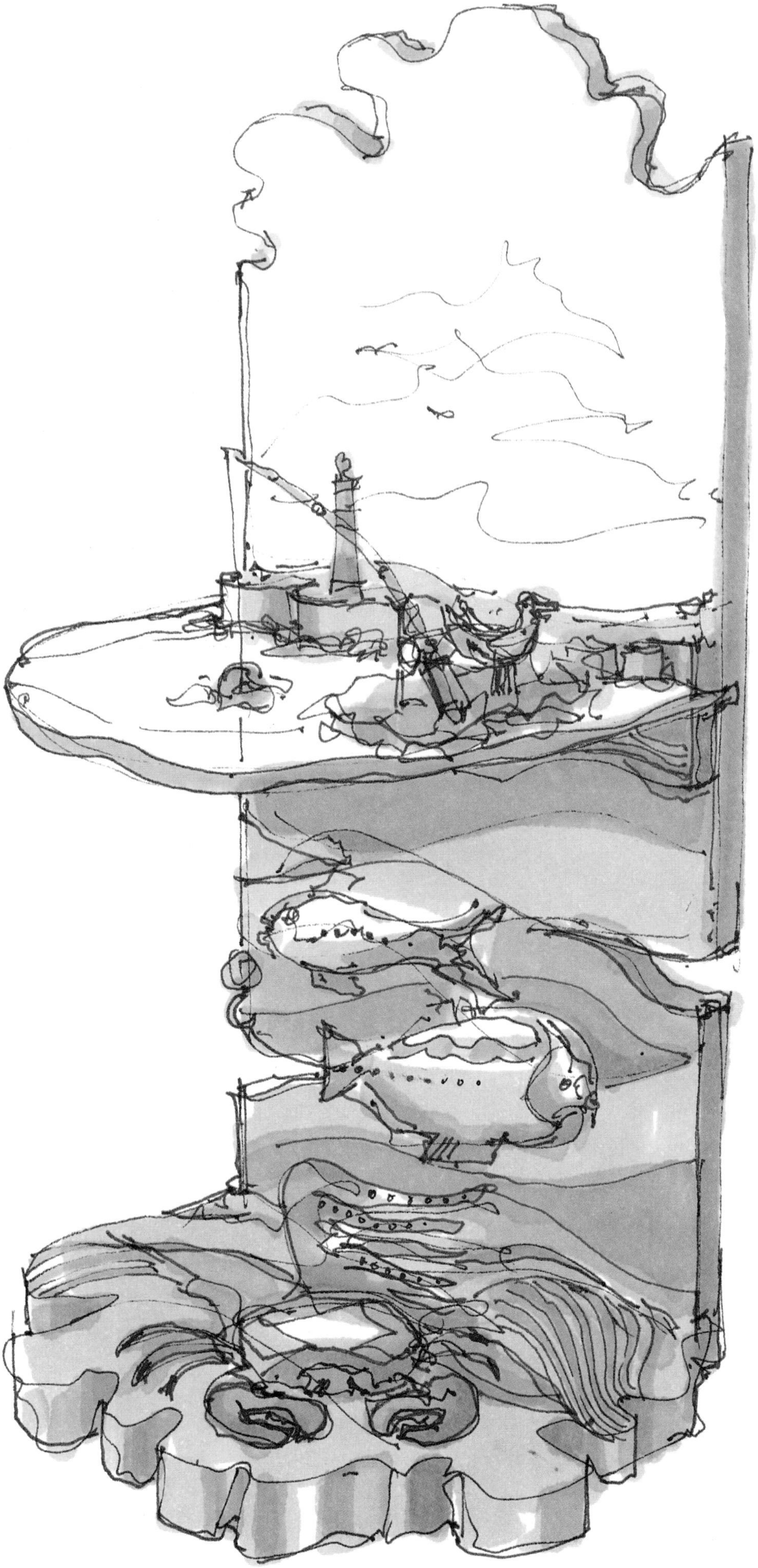

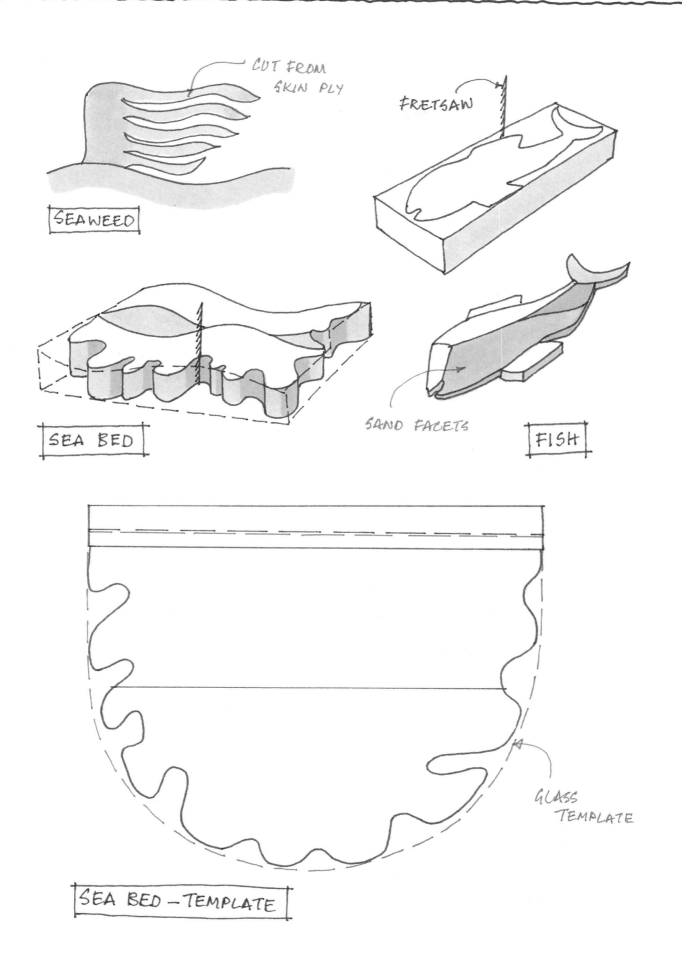

CUT FROM SKIN PLY

SEAWEED

FRETSAW

SEA BED

SAND FACETS

FISH

GLASS TEMPLATE

SEA BED — TEMPLATE

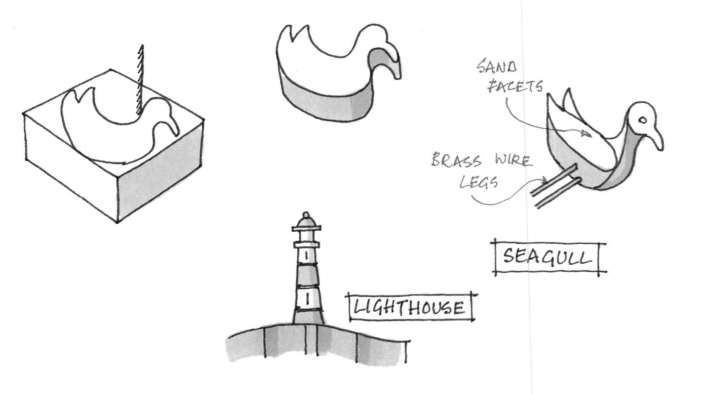

SAND
FACETS

BRASS WIRE
LEGS

SEAGULL

LIGHTHOUSE

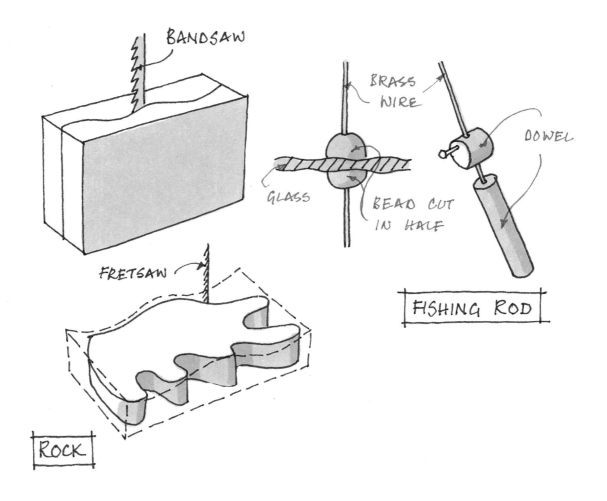

BANDSAW

BRASS WIRE

GLASS

BEAD CUT IN HALF

DOWEL

FISHING ROD

FRETSAW

ROCK

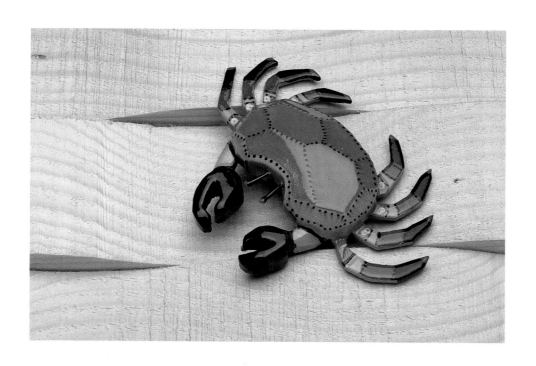

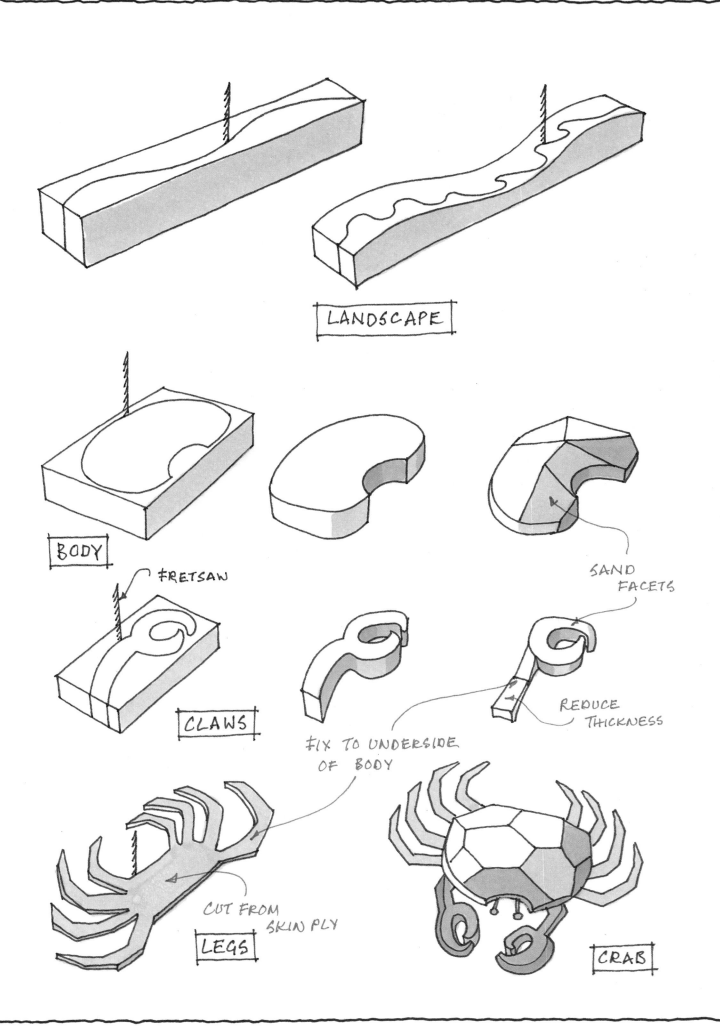

LANDSCAPE

BODY

CLAWS

FRETSAW

SAND FACETS

REDUCE THICKNESS

FIX TO UNDERSIDE OF BODY

CUT FROM SKIN PLY

LEGS

CRAB

RUNNING BEFORE THE STORM
HOME TIME
LETS GO

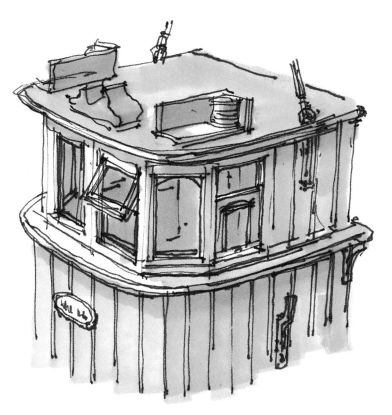

PLYMOUTH

33

a very POOR CATCH

- - - - - -

This scene shows the workings of the inside of a small coastal fishing boat. The boat has just landed its catch, hence the title, and the crew is enjoying a cup of tea in the forecastle. The captain has probably gone to the pub to drown his sorrows. At first the boat may look complicated but break it down into the individual elements and you will find it is easy to construct and parts are very similar to *Fishing Boat at Sea*. It is cut away on the starboard side to give a view below deck.

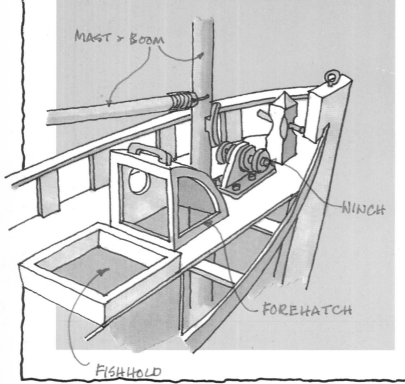

MAST & BOOM

WINCH

FOREHATCH

FISHHOLD

Guidelines for buying materials are given on page 10. All plans, elevations and templates are drawn to full size so that they can be traced directly off the page. Read through the instructions before starting and gather together all the materials you need. Remember it is easier to paint items before gluing them together. Make the glass case as described on page 48.

DIMENSIONS OF THE GLASS CASE
depth 8in (20cm), width 13in (33cm), height 11in (28cm).

1 Make the hull first, using the full-size plan (page 40) as a template. Cut the baseboard and transom from skin ply, the stem and stern posts from timber. Glue them together. Cut out bulkheads A and B from skin ply and fix them to the baseboard as shown. Cut out and attach the deck.

2 You now have the shape of the boat which should be rigid enough to accept the port side of the boat. Cut this using the template. Then glue the whole thing to the bulkheads, baseboard and deck. At this stage, fit the deck beams which provide the shape for the starboard side of the boat. Make ribs from strips of timber and attach them to the port side.

3 Make all the remaining elements, including the wheelhouse, ladder, winch, samson post and forehatch, using the diagrams on pages 42–3 as a guide. Some can be found in the first project *Fishing Boat at Sea* (page 18). Paint them and fit them to the hull.

4 Construct the engine from a block of wood using a fretsaw. Cut the basic shape with the wood flat on (see page 44) then turn the block and cut the more subtle vertical elements. Paint, then attach copper tubing and brass wire. The flywheel is made from a section of dowel. Don't forget the bank of switches (page 45).

5 Make the crew from wood and the teapot and cup from dowel and brass wire.

6 The boat is moored by a quay. Construct this next. First make a box from hardboard – the quay. Then cut the rocks for the harbour wall by sanding facets on the end of a length of timber then cutting it as shown in the diagram on page 46. Stick the rocks to the box, leaving a horizontal slot for the glass surface of the water.

7 Using cellulose car body filler, fix the hull of the boat to the top of a sheet of glass the same length as the dock wall. Add the keel below the glass, then fix the glass between the stones of the quay and into slots cut in the uprights of the glass case (see page 49).

8 Cut out and stick the sea bed using the instructions in *Fishing Boat at Sea* (page 17).

9 The crabs, fish and seaweed are the same as in *A Long Day's Fishing* (pages 24–31).

10 Finish by painting the boat in a colour of your choice, bearing in mind that fishing boats tend to be painted in bright primary colours.

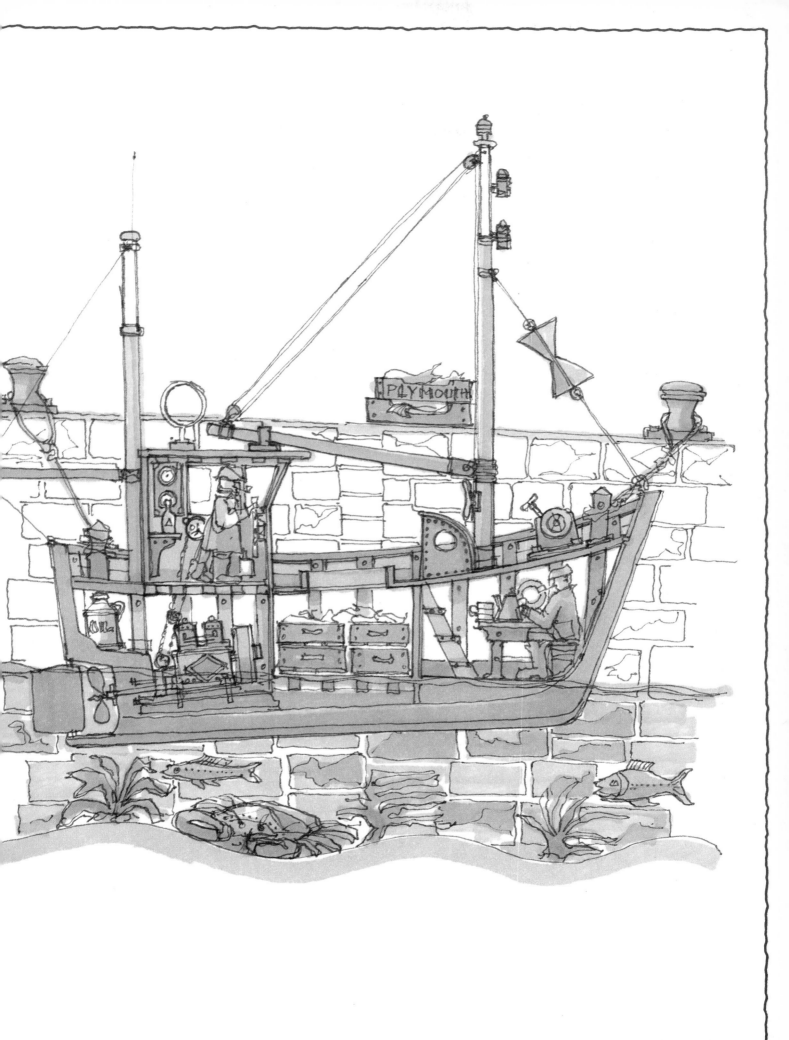

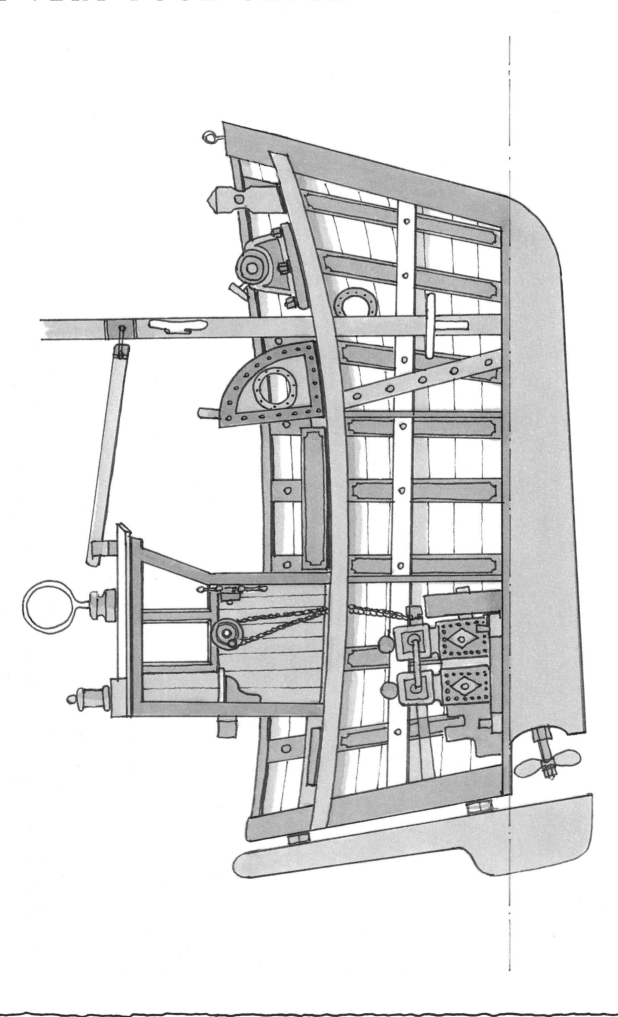

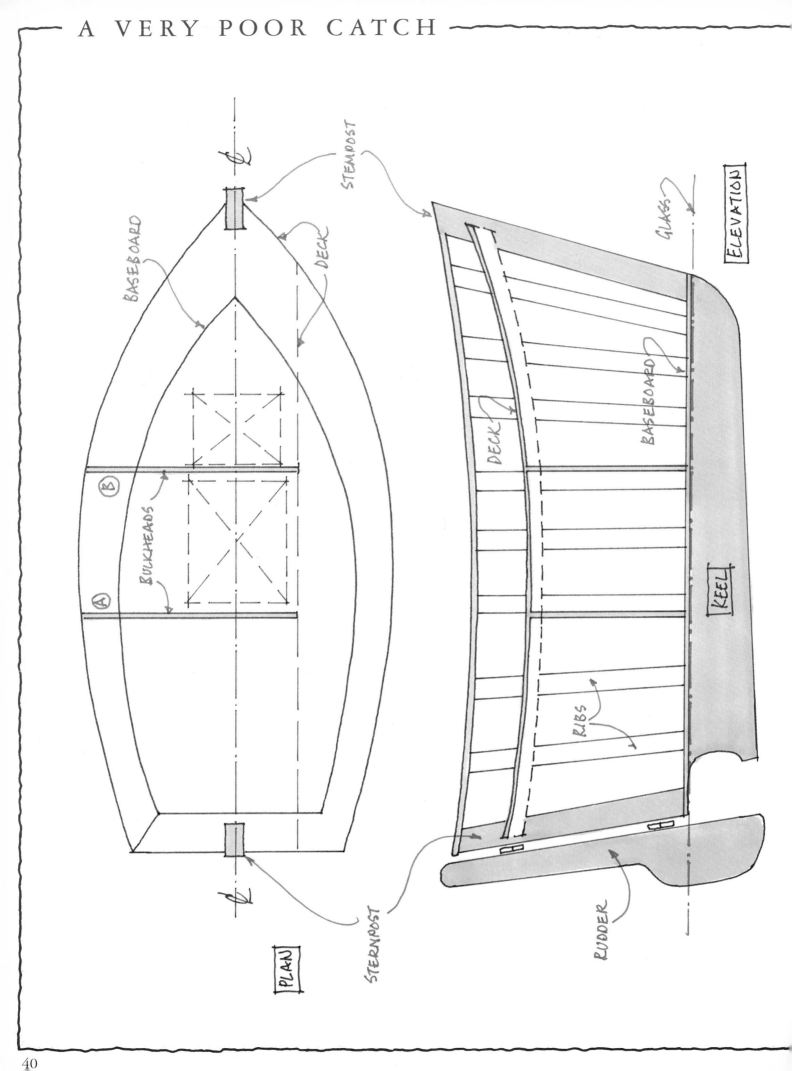

STERNPOST

DECK

BASEBOARD

PLAN

BULKHEADS

Ⓐ

Ⓑ

STERNPOST

ELEVATION

GLASS

DECK

BASEBOARD

KEEL

RIBS

RUDDER

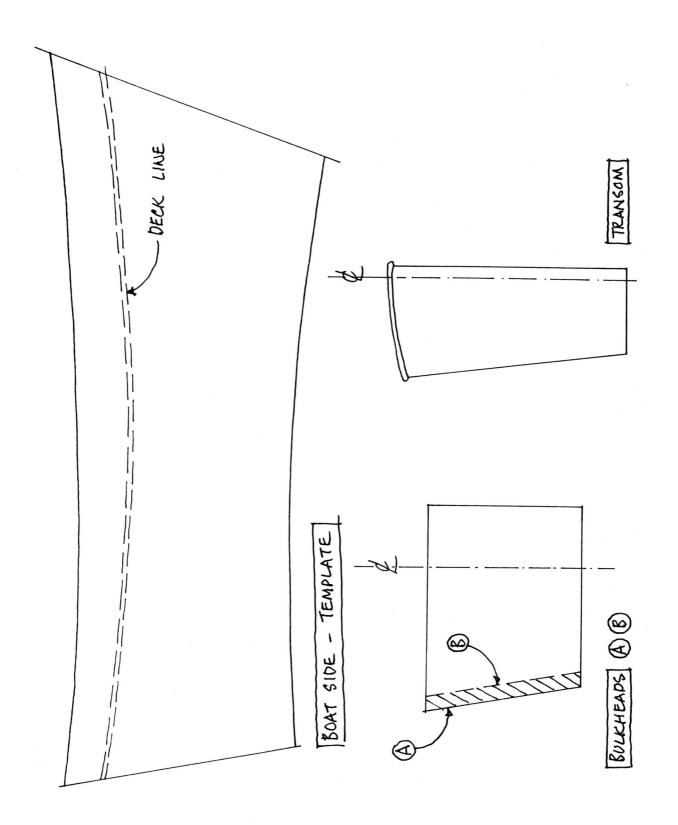

DECK LINE

BOAT SIDE - TEMPLATE

TRANSOM

BULKHEADS Ⓐ Ⓑ

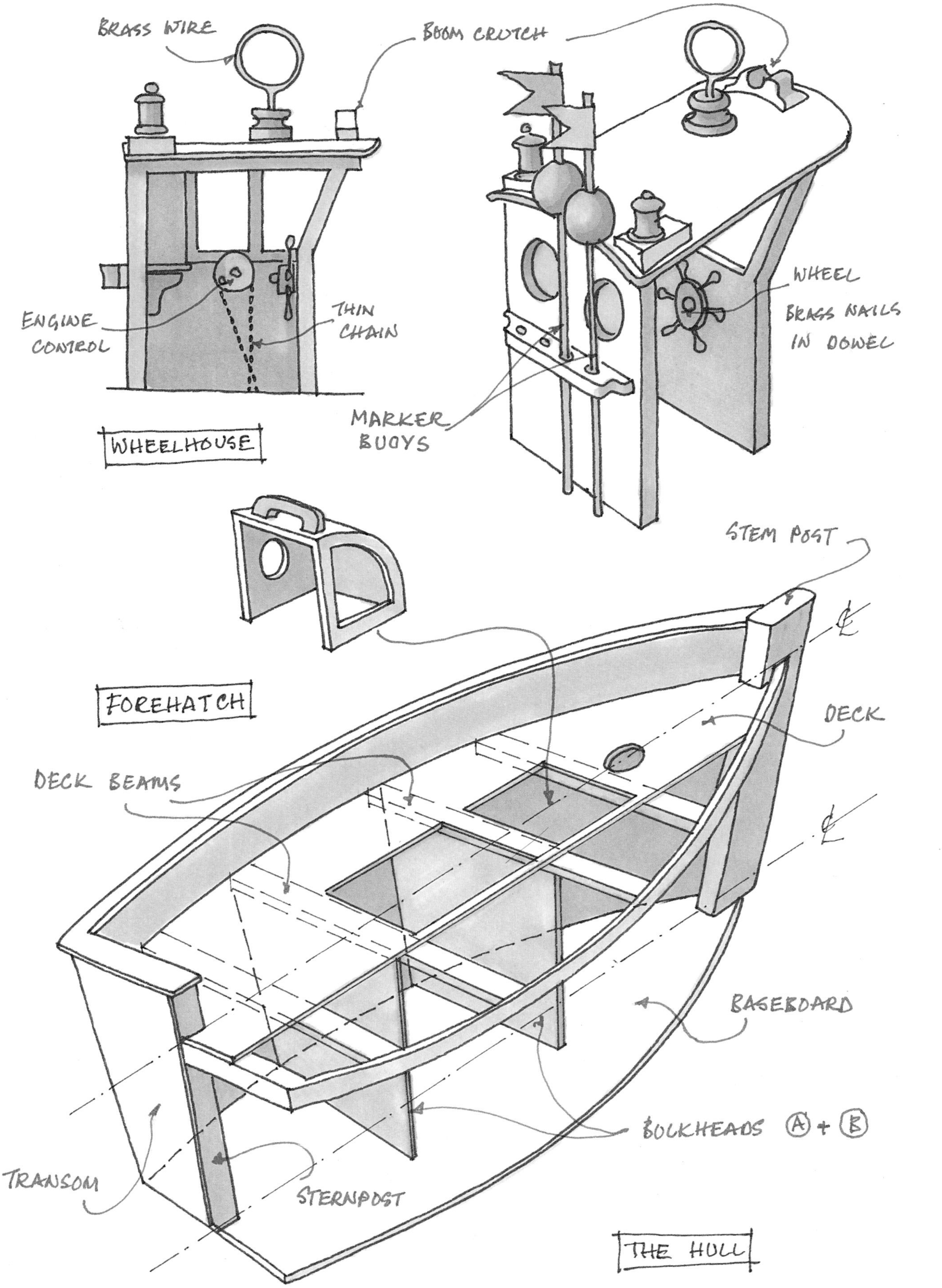

BRASS WIRE

BOOM CRUTCH

ENGINE CONTROL

THIN CHAIN

WHEEL

BRASS NAILS IN DOWEL

MARKER BUOYS

WHEELHOUSE

FOREHATCH

STEM POST

DECK

DECK BEAMS

BASEBOARD

BULKHEADS Ⓐ + Ⓑ

TRANSOM

STERNPOST

THE HULL

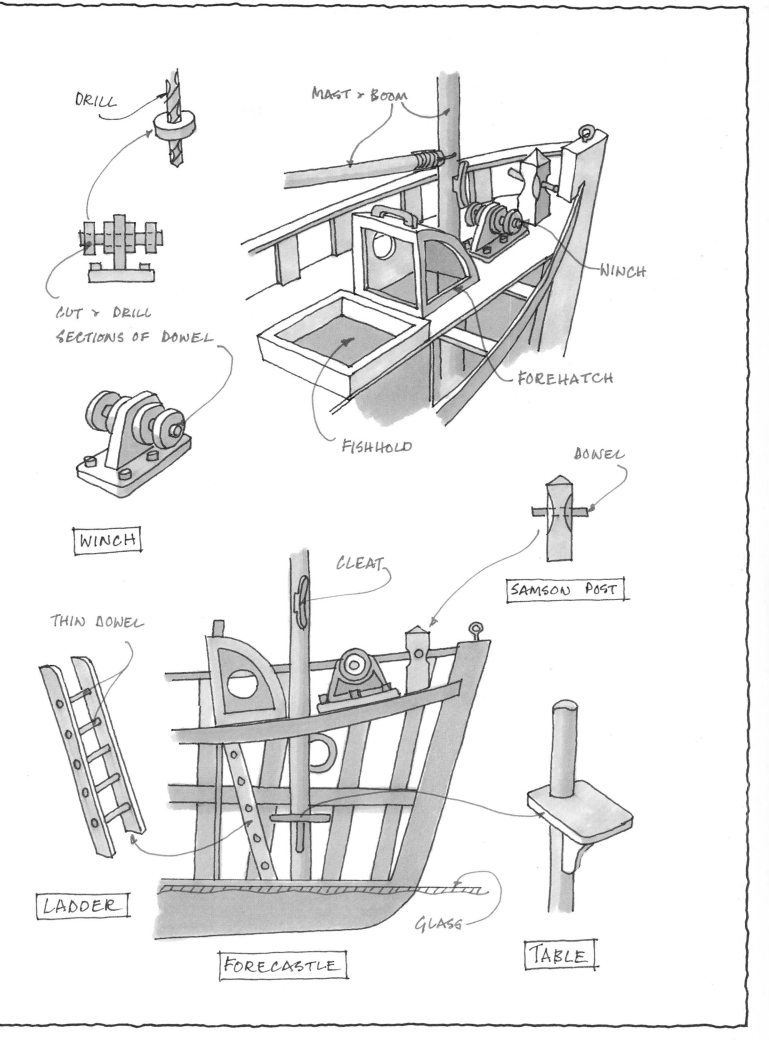

DRILL

CUT & DRILL
SECTIONS OF DOWEL

WINCH

MAST & BOOM

WINCH

FOREHATCH

FISHHOLD

DOWEL

SAMSON POST

CLEAT

THIN DOWEL

LADDER

GLASS

FORECASTLE

TABLE

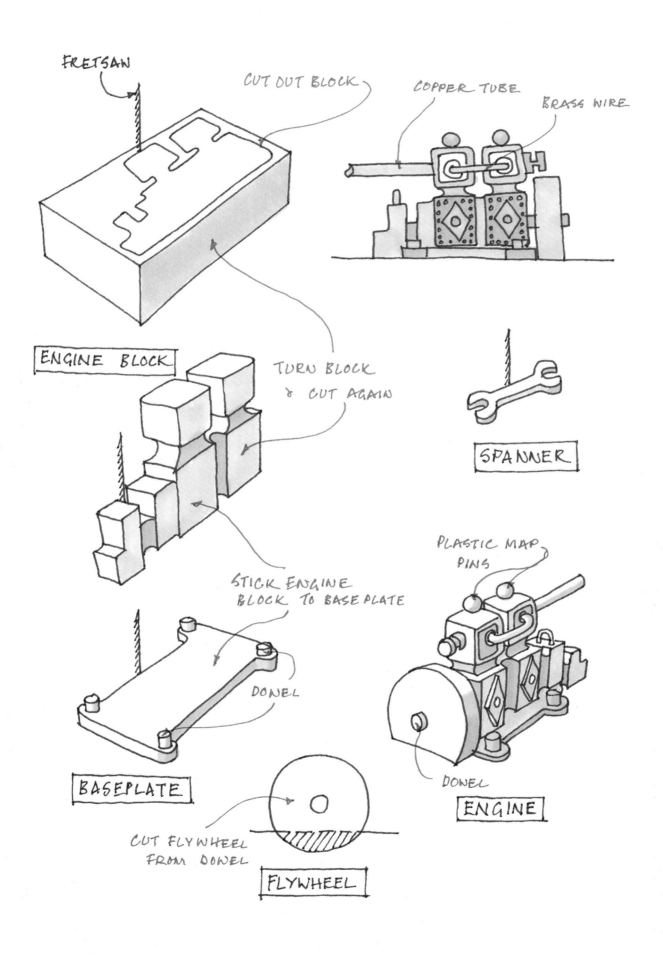

FRETSAW

CUT OUT BLOCK

COPPER TUBE

BRASS WIRE

ENGINE BLOCK

TURN BLOCK & CUT AGAIN

SPANNER

STICK ENGINE BLOCK TO BASEPLATE

PLASTIC MAP PINS

DONEL

BASEPLATE

DONEL

ENGINE

CUT FLYWHEEL FROM DONEL

FLYWHEEL

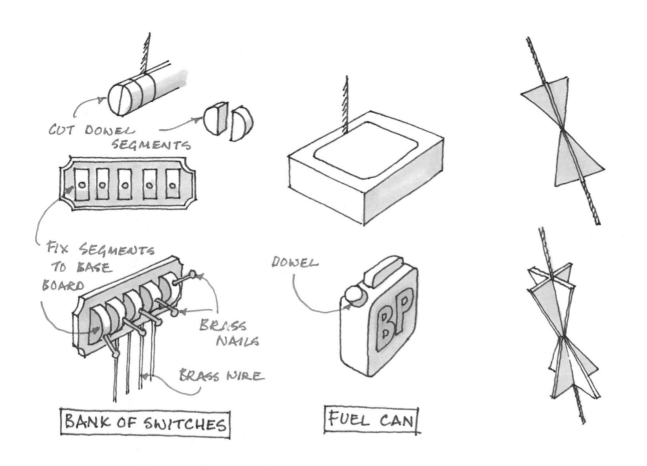

CUT DOWEL SEGMENTS

FIX SEGMENTS TO BASE BOARD

BRASS NAILS

BRASS WIRE

BANK OF SWITCHES

DOWEL

BP

FUEL CAN

PLYMOUTH

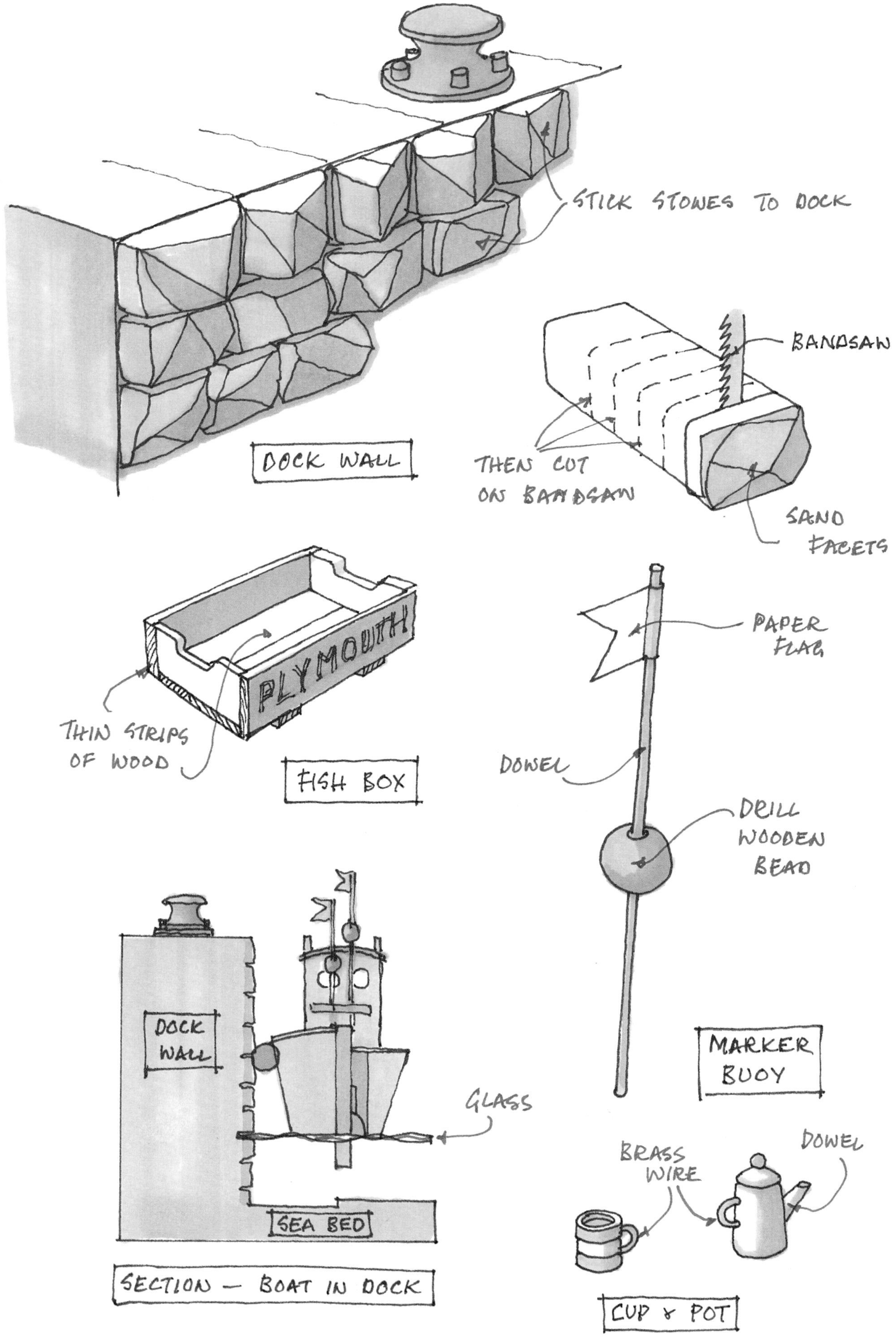

STICK STONES TO DOCK

DOCK WALL

BANDSAW

THEN CUT
ON BANDSAW

SAND
FACETS

THIN STRIPS
OF WOOD

PLYMOUTH

FISH BOX

PAPER
FLAG

DOWEL

DRILL
WOODEN
BEAD

MARKER
BUOY

DOCK
WALL

GLASS

SEA BED

SECTION — BOAT IN DOCK

BRASS
WIRE

DOWEL

CUP & POT

BEER
BOTTLE

WHEELHOUSE
SHELF

POT

CUP

TABLE

THE CREW

FILE TO SHAPE

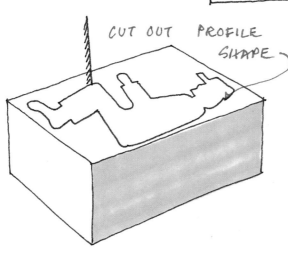

CUT OUT PROFILE
SHAPE

TURN OVER > CUT
AGAIN

MAKING GLASS CASES

All the glass cases in this book are constructed in the way described here; it is quite straightforward. Four pieces of ³/₄in (20mm) dowel cut to the required height of the case have lengthwise grooves cut in them in which to position the glass. They also each have a slot cut at the appropriate height to hold the panel of glass that is the surface of the sea. Once the various grooves and slots are cut the lengths of dowel are fitted into two pieces of ¹/₂in (12mm) MDF with holes drilled to accept them. The glass sides and hardboard back of the case are slid down the grooves first, then the surface of the sea is slid into the slots and, finally, the front glass panel is guided into place. The top is then screwed into place to hold the case together. To ensure a perfect fit for the glass, it is best to make the case first then take the whole thing to the glazier. The top and base of the case can be given routed edges to make them more elegant.

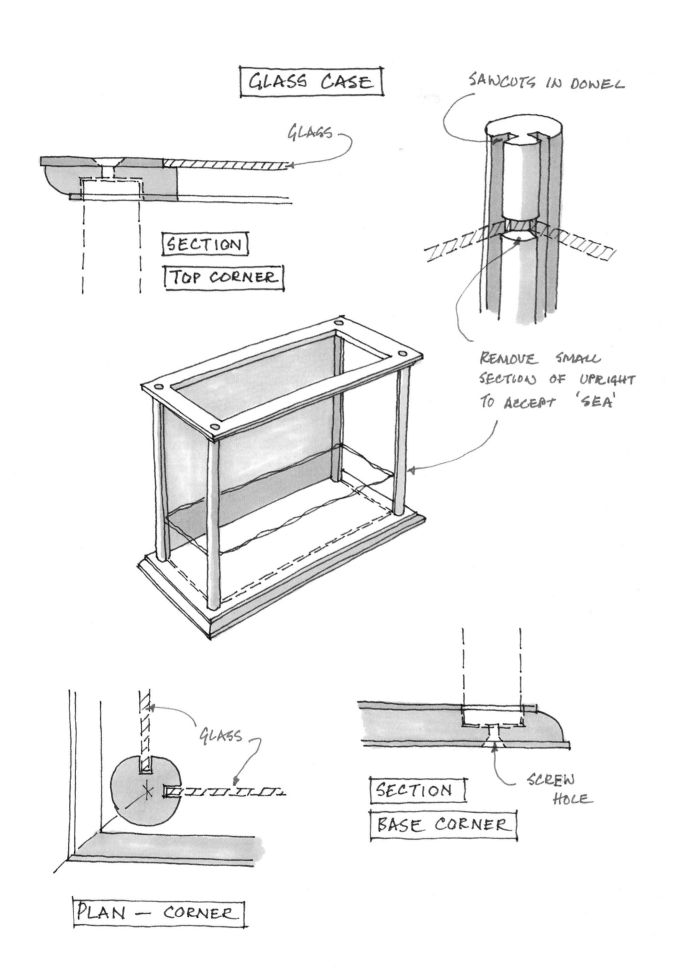

GLASS CASE

GLASS

SECTION
TOP CORNER

SAWCUTS IN DOWEL

REMOVE SMALL
SECTION OF UPRIGHT
TO ACCEPT 'SEA'

PLAN — CORNER

GLASS

SECTION
BASE CORNER

SCREW
HOLE

49

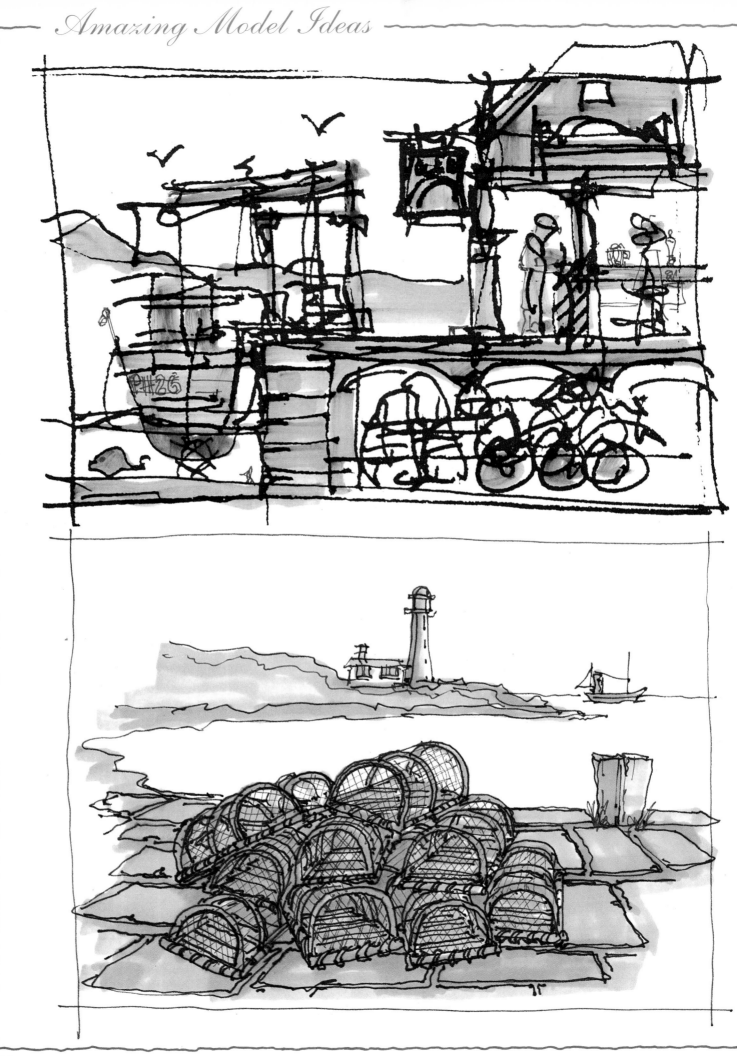

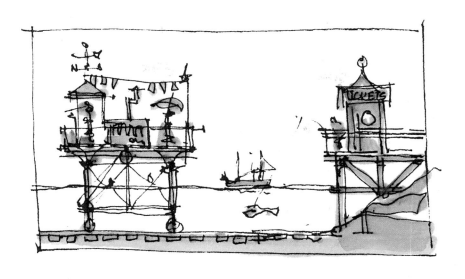

TOO HEAVY

high as a
KITE

A slight departure from the boat-in-water theme, this project depicts an airborne fantasy world of the past with champagne and horn gramophones. A sedate means of transport, far removed from the modern day desire for speed at all costs. The roof and one side are cut away to allow a view of the interior. Many of the familiar elements are also present – the surface of the sea, the lighthouse and the sea bed. However, all the detail is in the top part of the scene and the far away sea is less significant.

Guidelines for buying materials are given on page 10. All plans, elevations and templates are drawn to full size so that they can be traced directly off the page. Read through the instructions before starting and gather together all the materials you need. Remember it is easier to paint items before gluing them together. Make the glass case as described on page 48.

DIMENSIONS OF THE GLASS CASE
depth 10in (25cm), width 15in (38cm),
height 24in (60cm).

1 Make the gondola first, using the front and side view drawings as templates. Use skin ply for the floor, side and front. The side and front are then clad with small strips of timber. Make the back from thin strips of timber, glued to two curved pieces of skin ply as shown.

2 Next cut the skids, gondola supports and engine mounts (page 58) from skin ply. Drill large holes in them, as shown, and attach thin card to the edges. Paint as necessary and then glue them to the gondola.

3 The balloon is made from two pieces of 4 x 1in (100 x 25mm) timber planed to shape, as shown (page 58), and then glued together. A solid piece of timber forms the flat back end of the balloon. The first facets of its nose cone can now be planed, then add two solid sections of timber to make the final facets of the nose.

4 Make the two engines. Turn a piece of 1in (25mm) dowel on a lathe to form the main plug of the engine. Then cut and glue various different thicknesses of dowel as shown. Paint the engine and attach the details – brass nails, copper tubing and plastic map pins. The finished engine can now be glued to the engine mounts. Repeat for the other engine.

5 The elements of the interior – the anemometer, table, gramophone, stove, hod and chair – should now be made, following the diagrams and painting as you go. The stove is made from a turned piece of $^3/_4$in (20mm) dowel, brass nails and a section of copper tubing, the hod is a piece of $^1/_2$in (12mm) dowel, and the gramophone horn is turned from $^3/_4$in (20mm) dowel.

6 Cut out the flying seagull from a scrap of timber and mount it on a piece of piano wire fitted to the underside of the gondola. The seagull sitting on the roof of the gondola is from *A Long Day's Fishing* (page 29).

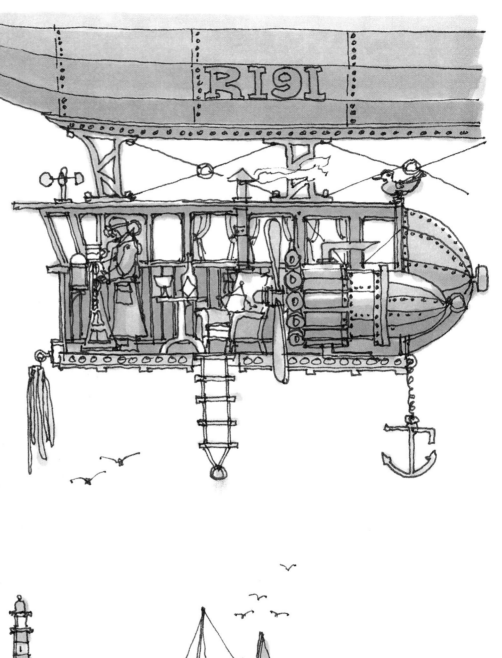

7 The anchor and chain which, like the flying seagull, hang below the gondola can be purchased from any model shop. The chain is strengthened with piano wire to make it rigid so that it can be bent as if blown by the wind.

8 Make the sea bed, glass sea surface, island and lighthouse as described in previous projects.

9 The captain and the passenger can be made from scraps of wood and dowel (see page 47).

10 Paint the background with clouds and, perhaps, a similar distant passing airship. Make the glass case and attach the model to the top board then lower it into the case and screw in place.

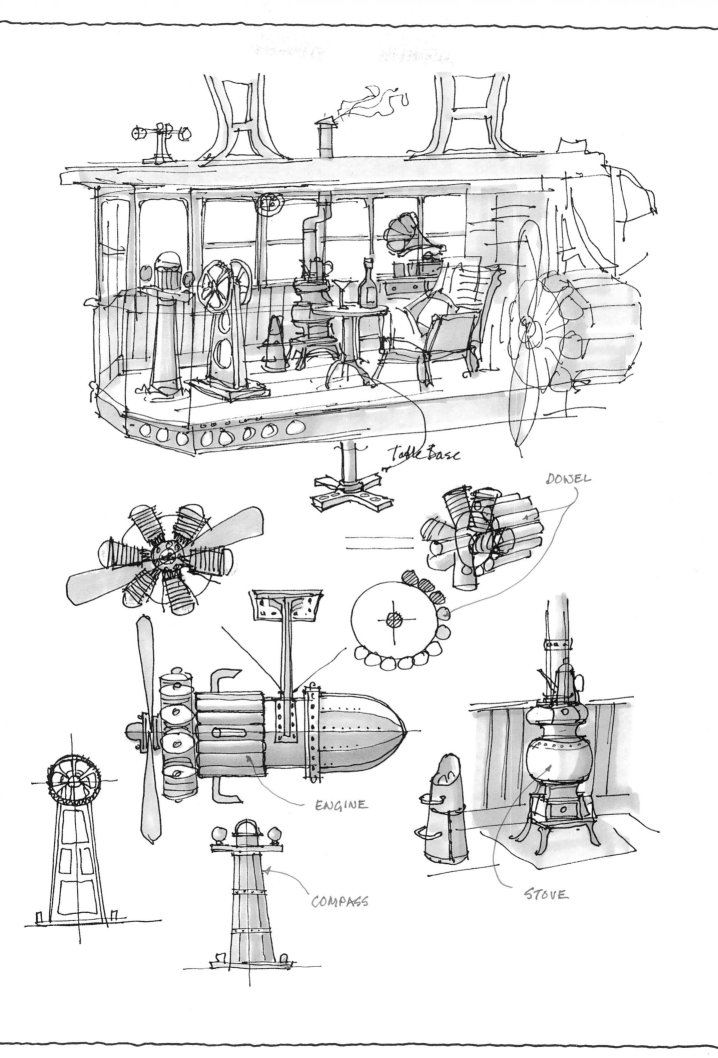

Table Base

DOWEL

ENGINE

COMPASS

STOVE

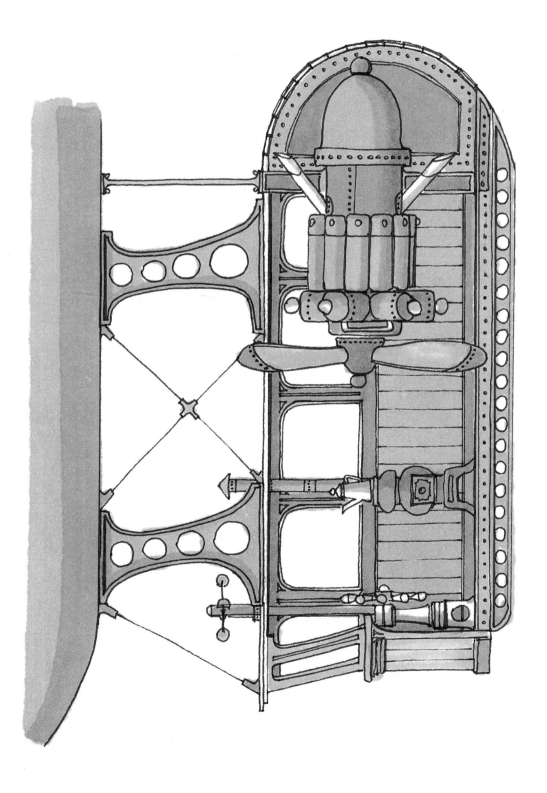

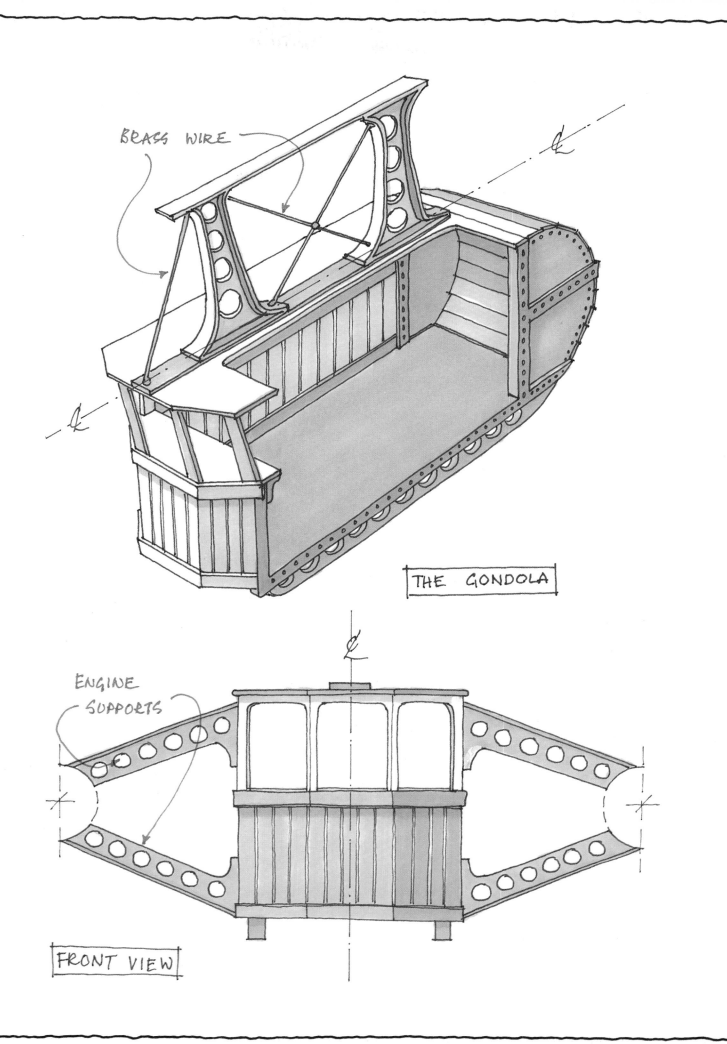

BRASS WIRE

THE GONDOLA

ENGINE SUPPORTS

FRONT VIEW

57

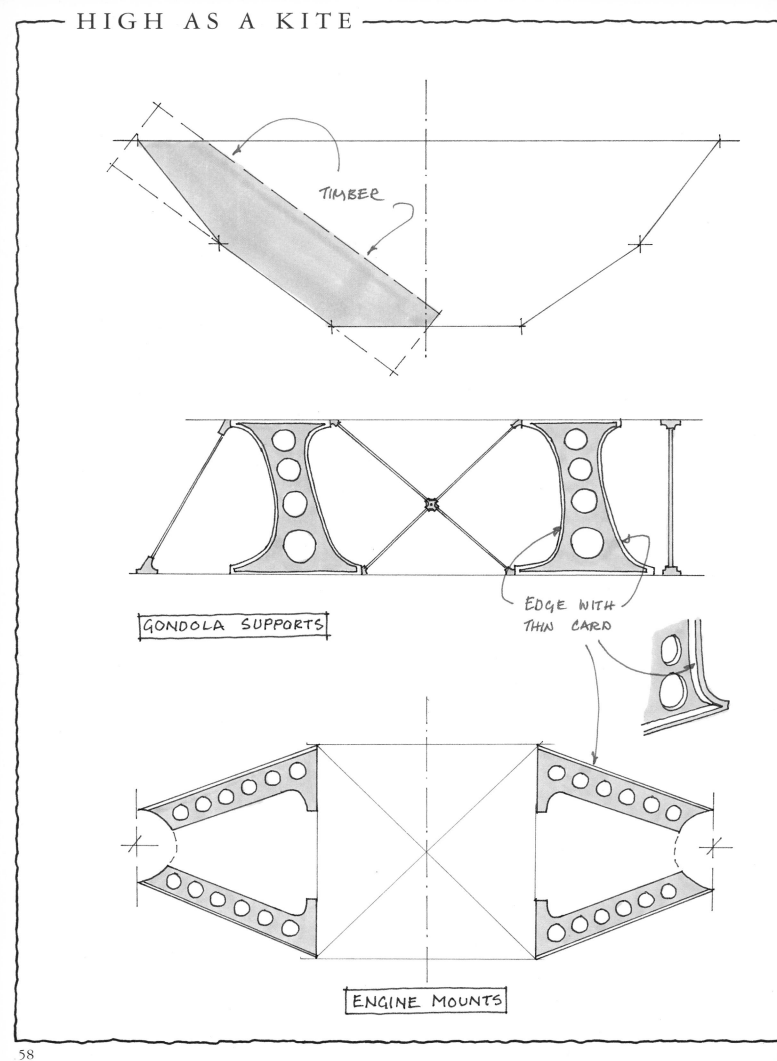

TIMBER

GONDOLA SUPPORTS

EDGE WITH THIN CARD

ENGINE MOUNTS

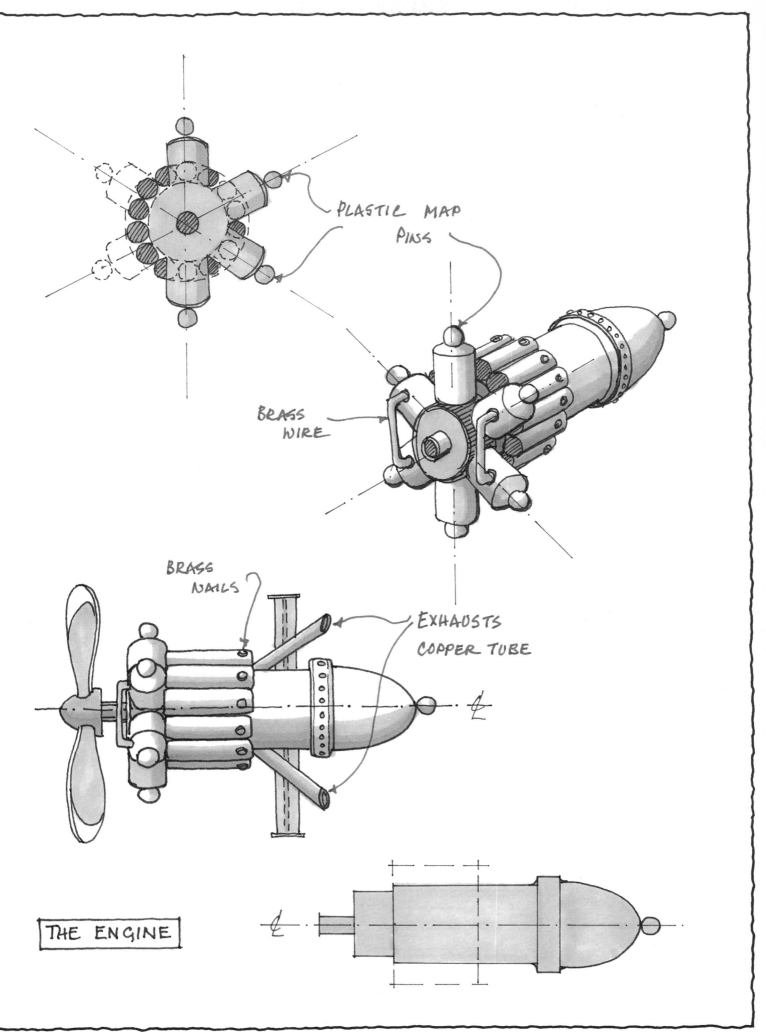

PLASTIC MAP PINS

BRASS WIRE

BRASS NAILS

EXHAUSTS COPPER TUBE

THE ENGINE

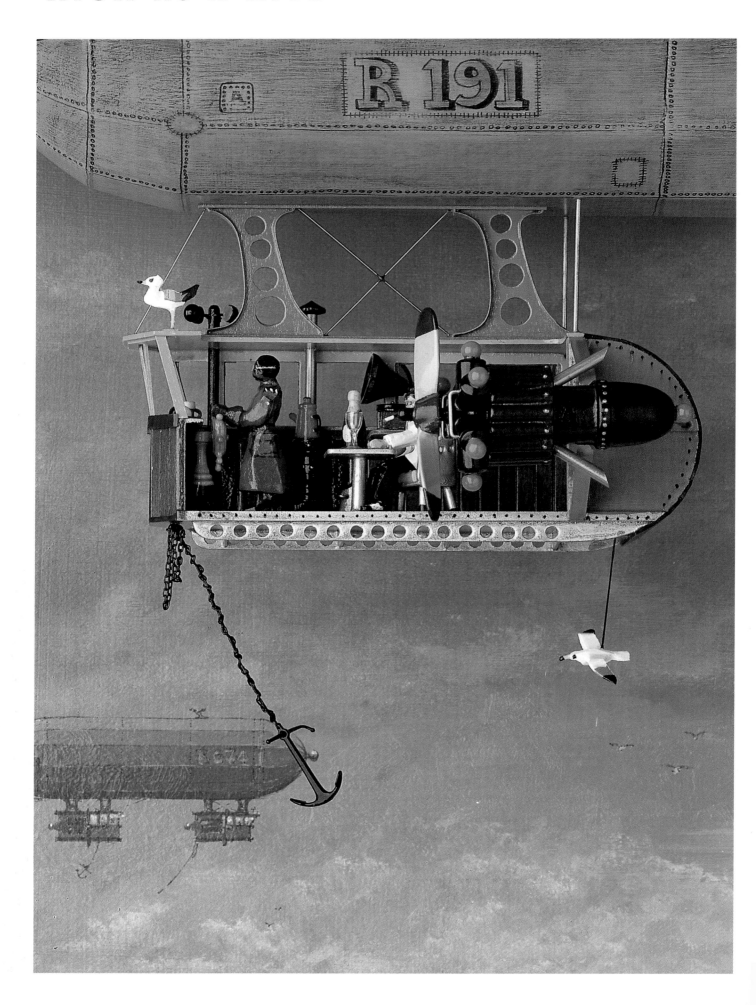

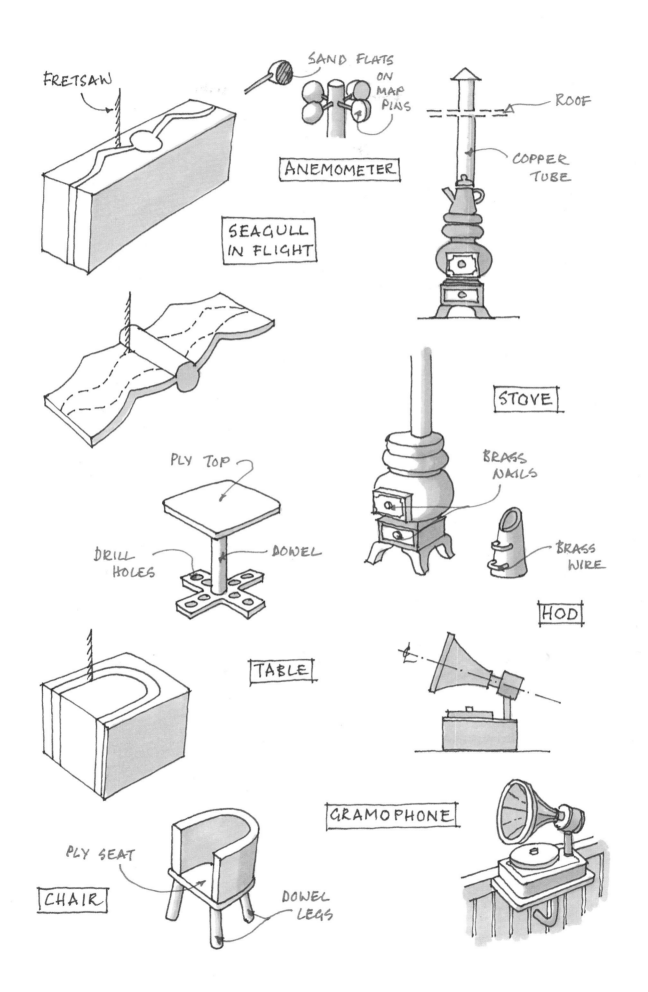

FRETSAW

SAND FLATS ON MAP PINS

ANEMOMETER

ROOF

COPPER TUBE

SEAGULL IN FLIGHT

STOVE

PLY TOP

BRASS NAILS

DRILL HOLES

DOWEL

BRASS WIRE

HOD

TABLE

PLY SEAT

GRAMOPHONE

CHAIR

DOWEL LEGS

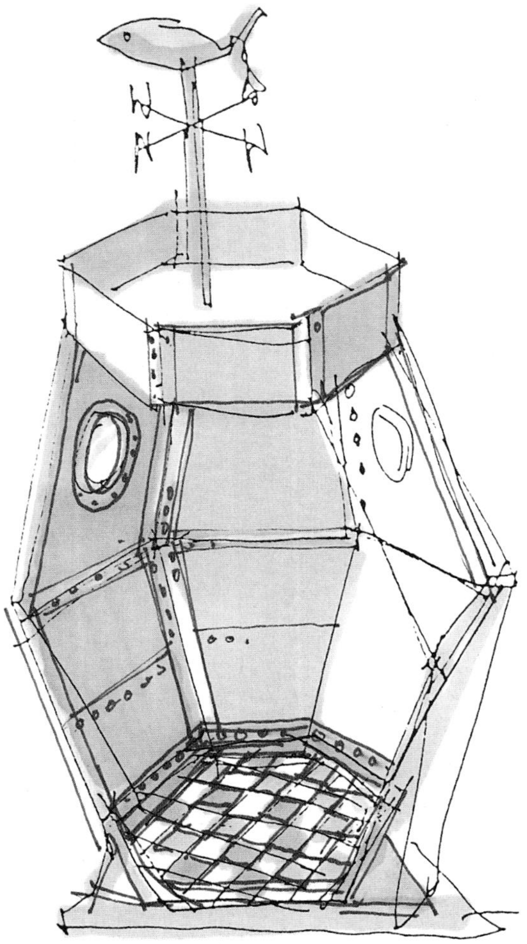

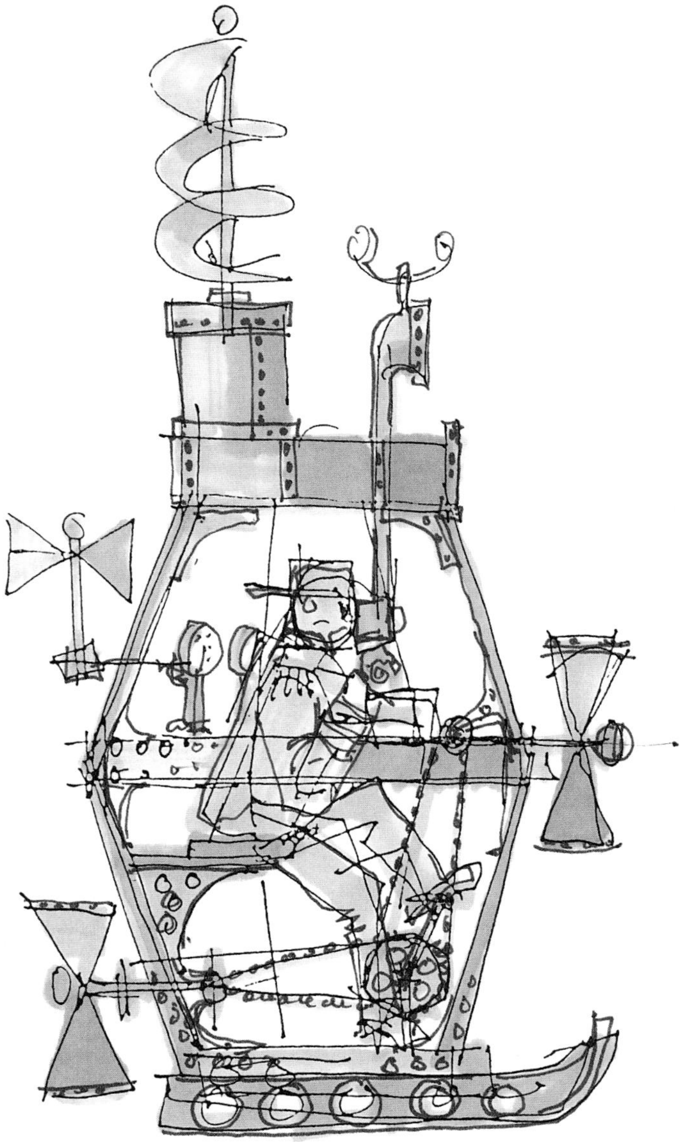

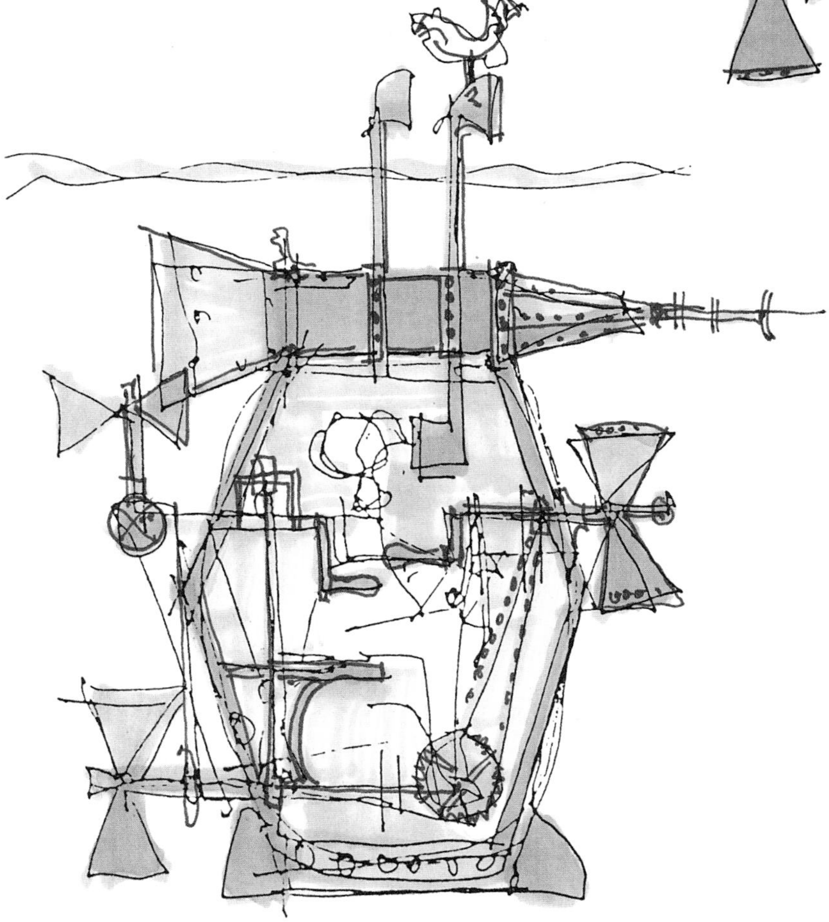

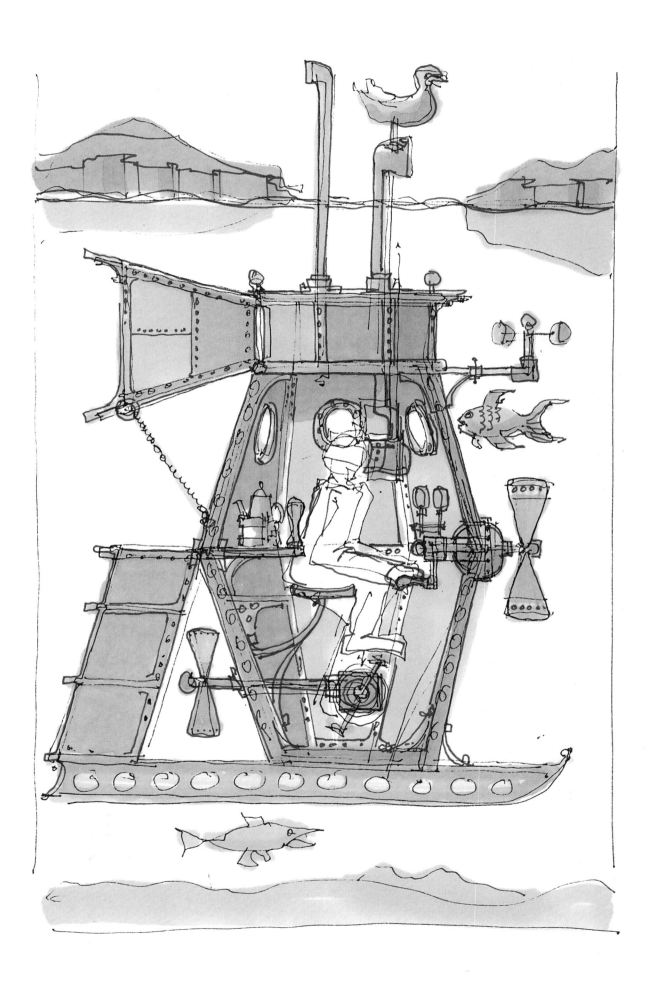

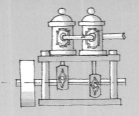

a little late for
HENLEY

This steam launch is typical of those that can still be found on the River Thames. The captain and his guest are on a jaunt down the river but seem to have taken a wrong turn and are now floating through a tropical jungle. Unperturbed, he is enjoying a cup of tea while she relaxes in the shade of her canopy, drinking champagne. A serpent lurks in the still waters below.

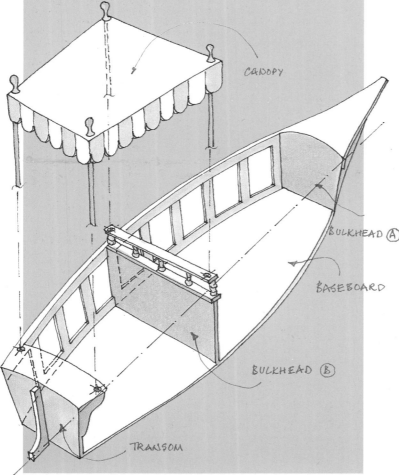

CANOPY

BULKHEAD Ⓐ

BASEBOARD

BULKHEAD Ⓑ

TRANSOM

Guidelines for buying materials are given on page 10. All plans, elevations and templates are drawn to full size so that they can be traced directly off the page. Read through the instructions before starting and gather together all the materials you need. Remember it is easier to paint items before gluing them together. Make the glass case as described on page 48.

DIMENSIONS OF THE GLASS CASE
depth 11½in (29cm), width 15½in (39cm), height 12in (30cm).

1 Cut out the baseboard of the hull from skin ply using the full-sized drawing (page 71) as a template. Cut transom and bulkheads A and B from skin ply, and glue to the baseboard in the positions shown in the plan.

2 Using extra thin ply cut the port side of the hull and glue it to bulkheads A and B, and the transom.

3 Now cut and add the fore and aft decks. Use extra thin ply for the small front section of the starboard side of the hull and glue it in place.

4 Make ribs from strips of thin timber and fix to the inside of the hull.

5 Construct the canopy from thin ply and fit it on to the aft deck and bulkhead B with brass wire uprights. The railings on bulkhead B are made from small turnings, available at model shops, and are topped with a small timber rail.

6 Make the rudder in two sections sticking the lower piece below the glass water's surface with cellulose car body filler. Attach it to the boat in the same way. The keel should also be positioned below the hull on the lower surface of the glass and the plastic propeller is glued to it.

7 Next come the engine and boiler. Use a lathe to turn the boiler and chimney from a section of 1in (25mm) dowel. Form the bands around the boiler at the same time. Hammer brass pins into these bands to look like rivets. The cylinders, made from sections of dowel, also need turning. When you paint the boiler include vertical lines to simulate timber cladding. Use brass wire and thin copper tubing to finish.

8 Stacking 4 sheets of skin ply at a time, cut out the grass, trees and undergrowth. Clean them up with sandpaper and paint them. Fit them into the glass case as shown in the section (page 74). Make the serpent from a length of timber and support it from the river bed on thin piano wire.

9 Cut the captain and his passenger from timber as shown on page 47. They must be carved by hand into shape, then painted.

10 All the other elements, such as the table, the captain's chair and the shovel can now be made. Use dowel and follow instructions in the previous projects for making things like the cup of tea and the seagull. Don't forget the sign post.

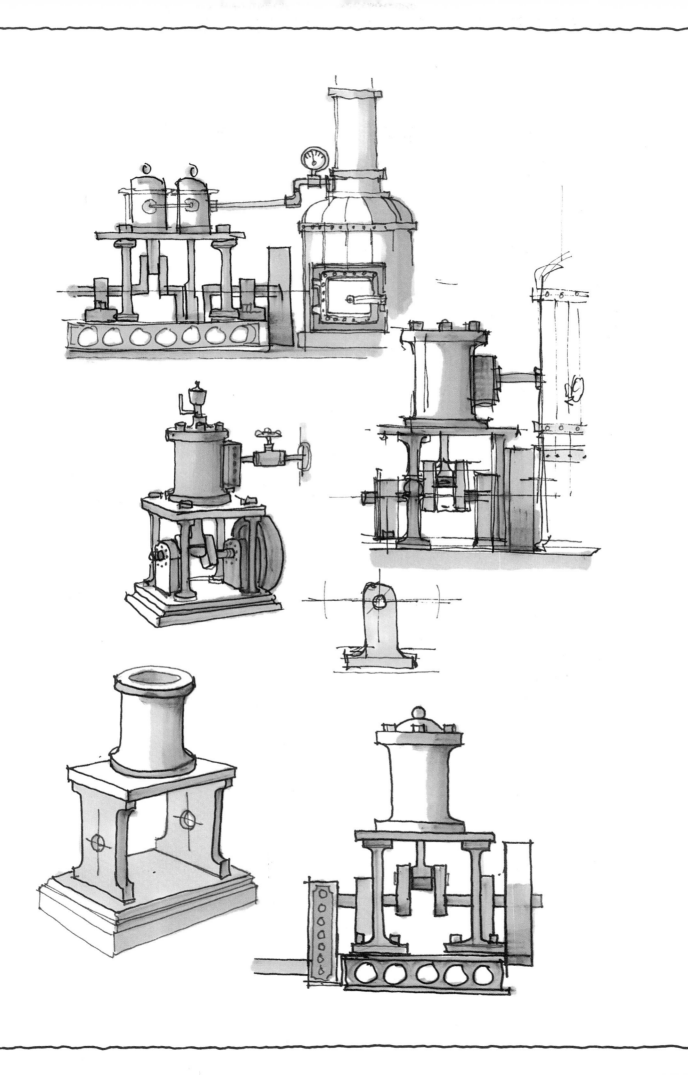

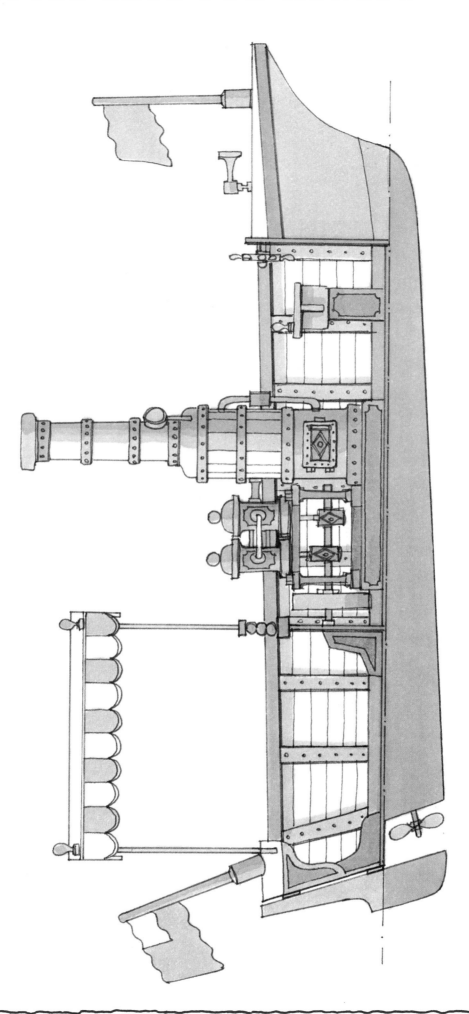

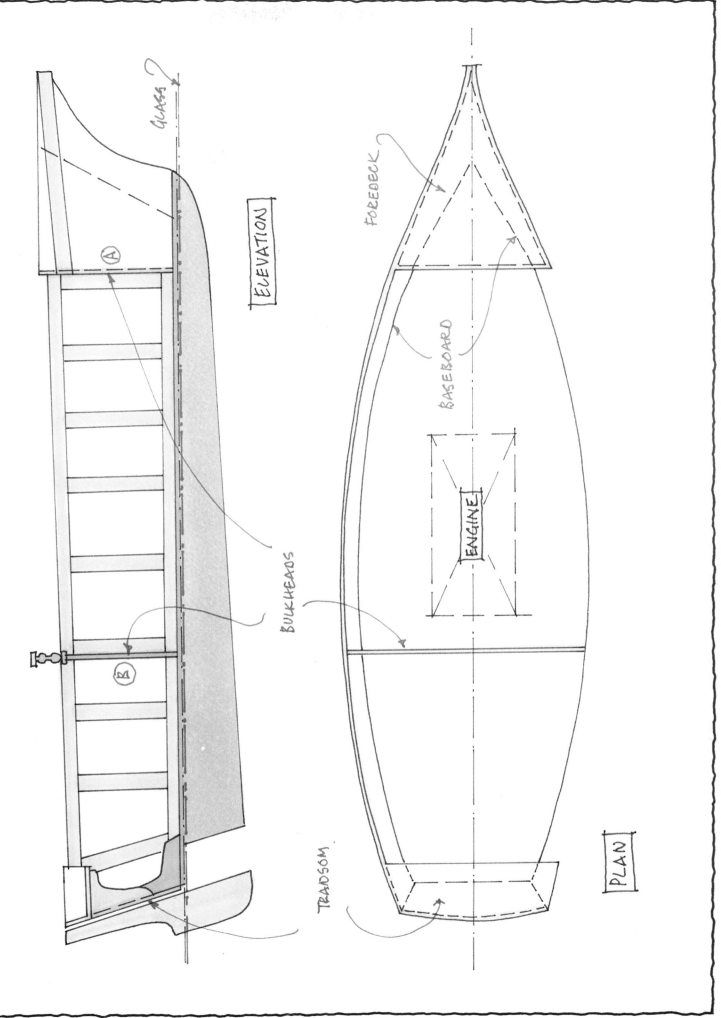

GLASS

ELEVATION

Ⓐ

Ⓑ

BULKHEADS

TRANSOM

FOREDECK

BASEBOARD

ENGINE

PLAN

71

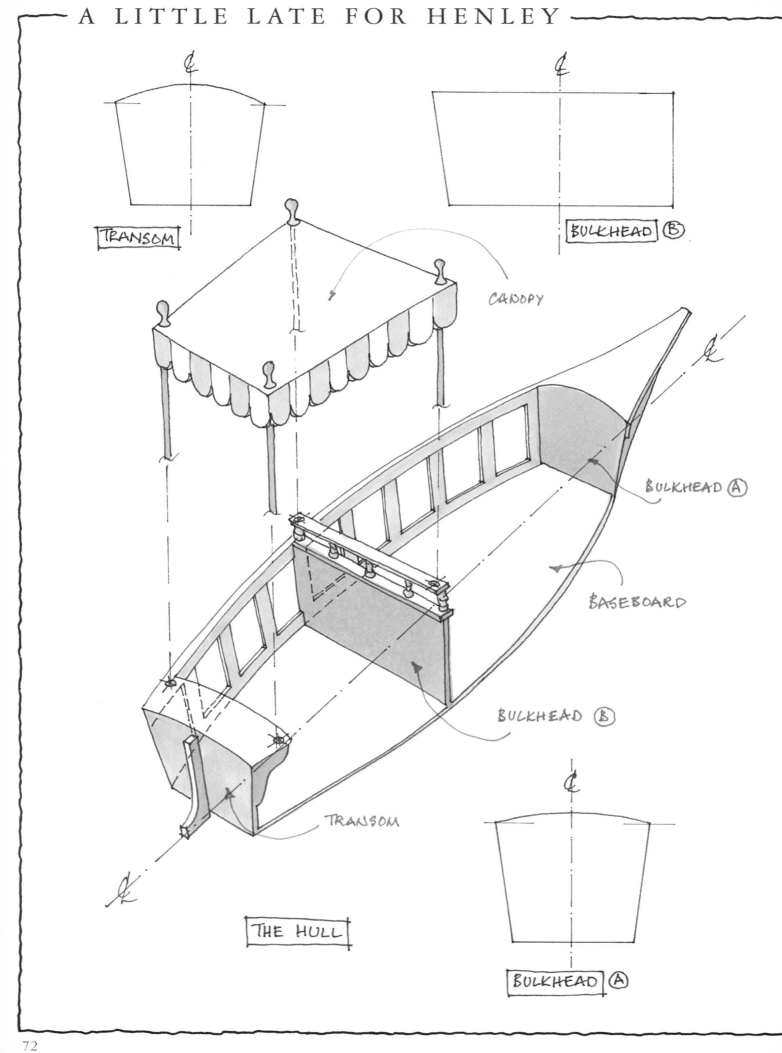

TRANSOM

BULKHEAD Ⓑ

CANOPY

BULKHEAD Ⓐ

BASEBOARD

BULKHEAD Ⓑ

TRANSOM

THE HULL

BULKHEAD Ⓐ

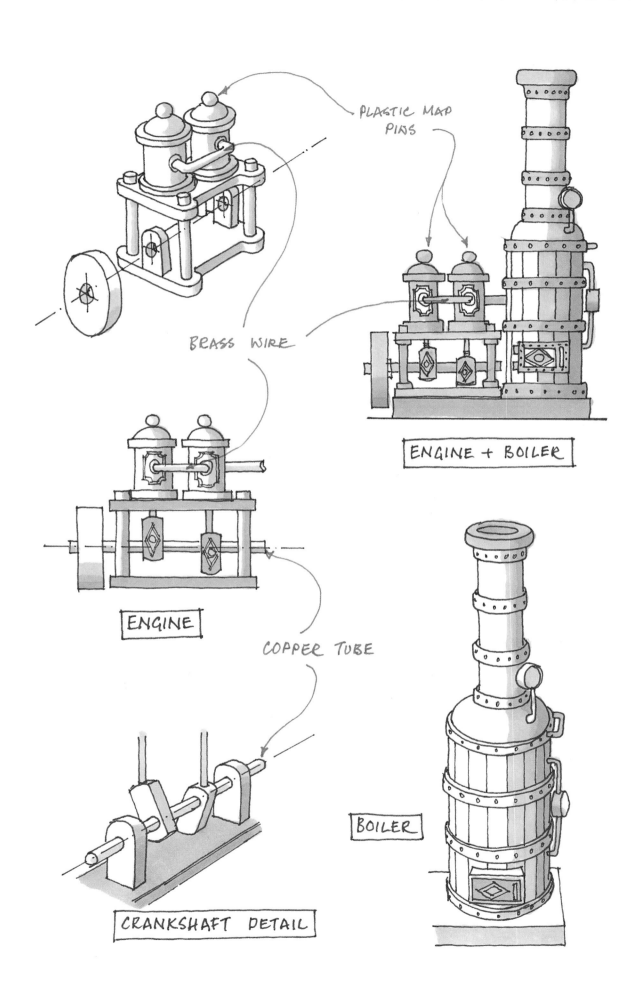

PLASTIC MAP PINS

BRASS WIRE

ENGINE + BOILER

ENGINE

COPPER TUBE

CRANKSHAFT DETAIL

BOILER

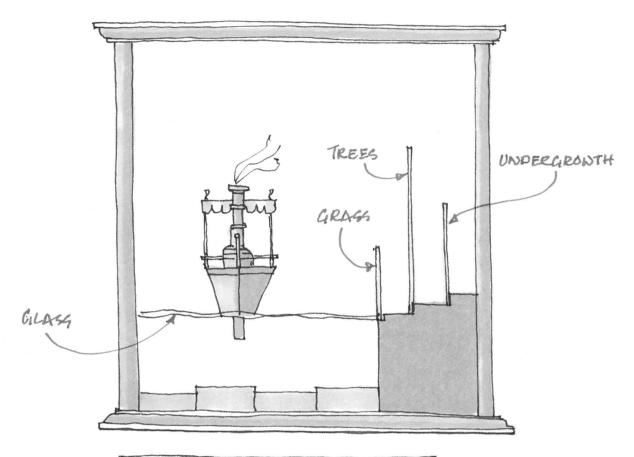

SECTION — GLASS CAGE

THE JUNGLE

GRASS

TREE

FRETSAW

SAND FACETS

SERPENT

BRASS WIRE

PIANO WIRE

STACK CUT
4 SHEETS OF PLY

UNDERGROWTH

75

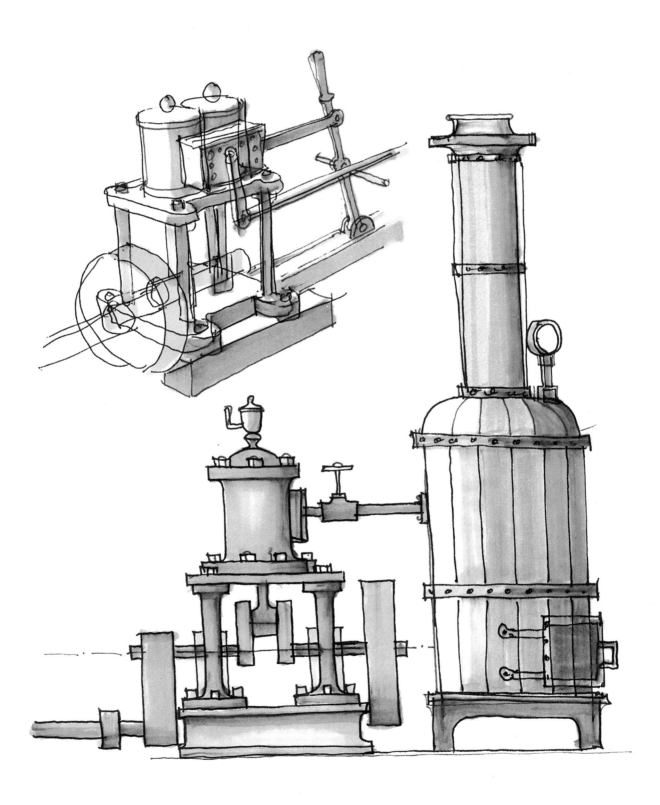

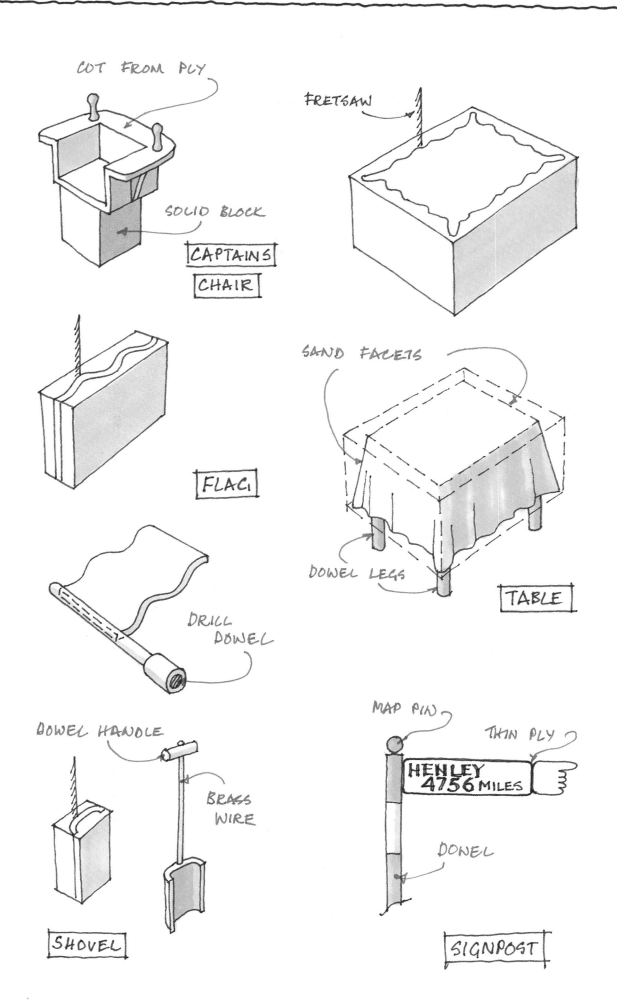

CUT FROM PLY

SOLID BLOCK

CAPTAINS
CHAIR

FRETSAW

FLAG

DRILL
DOWEL

SAND FACETS

DOWEL LEGS

TABLE

DOWEL HANDLE

BRASS
WIRE

SHOVEL

MAP PIN

THIN PLY

HENLEY
4756 MILES

DOWEL

SIGNPOST

OTTER
BOARDS

NET

tea-break off
DRAKE'S
ISLAND
- - - - - - -

In this exploration of life under
the sea, a submarine is shown passing
Drake's Island on the way to its home
port of Devonport. Inside the captain is
on watch, while his crew enjoys a good
read and some tea and cake. A seagull
hitches a ride on the periscope.

All is well.

Guidelines for buying materials are given on page 10. All plans, elevations and templates are drawn to full size so that they can be traced directly off the page. Read through the instructions before starting and gather together all the materials you need. Remember it is easier to paint items before gluing them together. Make the glass case as described on page 48.

DIMENSIONS OF THE GLASS CASE
depth 11½in (29cm), width 15½in (39cm), height 12in (30cm).

1 First make the hull of the submarine, which is a series of cut out ribs fixed to a central spine, rather like the ribcage of a fish. Use the full-size sections and elevations as a guide. Cut the spine from a strip of ¼in (6mm) timber and drill holes as shown. Then cut the ribs from thin ply using the section templates 1 to 8, and glue these to the spine. Only one set of ribs is necessary as the other side of the submarine is left open for a better view.

2 Next cut and fit the floors, gluing them on to the flattened lower side of the ribs and the central spine.

3 Use dowel turned on a lathe to make the nose cone, then glue it to the front bulkhead. Hammer brass nails into the nosecone to simulate rivets.

4 Cut the companionway openings (section A-A) into the fore and aft bulkheads of the conning tower then fit them in place. Note that the openings are edged with thin card. Instructions for the handles are on page 18.

5 Paint the ribs and add the details of the forward compartment – the torpedo, the crew and his tea – before fitting the outer skin of the submarine, which is made from thin card. The torpedo is made from ¹/₂in (12mm) dowel turned on a lathe.

6 The periscope comes next. This has a central shaft of copper tube with the eyepiece and external lens, made of dowel and wood, fixed to it. Use thin chain and pulleys for the raising mechanism.

7 The engine is made with elements that are similar to those used in projects such as *A Very Poor Catch* (page 44). Basically it is a shaped piece of wood and turned dowel, painted carefully then fitted with brass wire and copper tube and positioned in the engine room. The propeller is plastic and has a drive shaft of copper tube. The rudder is skin ply and dowel.

8 The sea bed is made in two parts (see section through case), the rear falls in a 45° slope and the foreground is flat. Make the bed with small lengths of timber cut with the bandsaw (see page 17). Fix this to a back board of ¹/₄in (6mm) MDF, then fix the submarine from the back using two lengths of dowel drilled into the 45° slope of the sea bed. Add a piece of glass for the water's surface. This is attached with car body filler.

9 Turn dowel on a lathe to make the two buoys. Then cut them in half at an angle. Fix them above and below the water's surface with car body filler. The angle simulates the passing of the tide. Chains tether the buoys to the sea bed.

10 Make Drake's Island, with its flag, and the distant landscape and attach them to the glass and back board with car body filler.

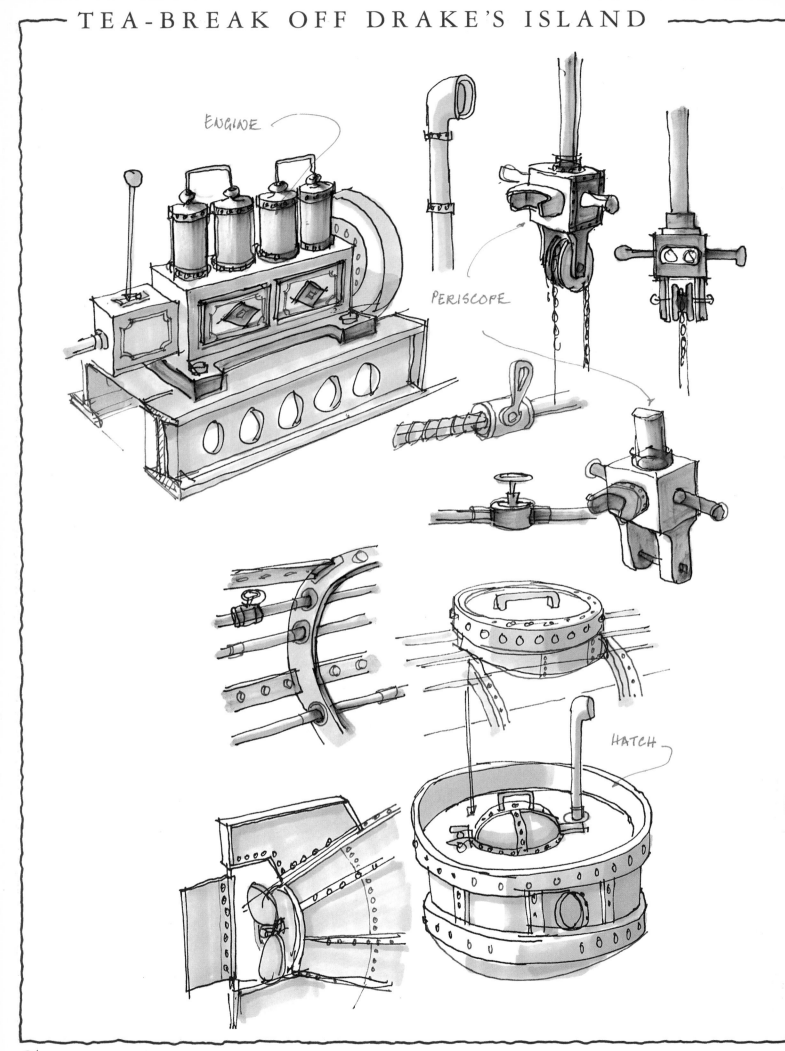

ENGINE

PERISCOPE

HATCH

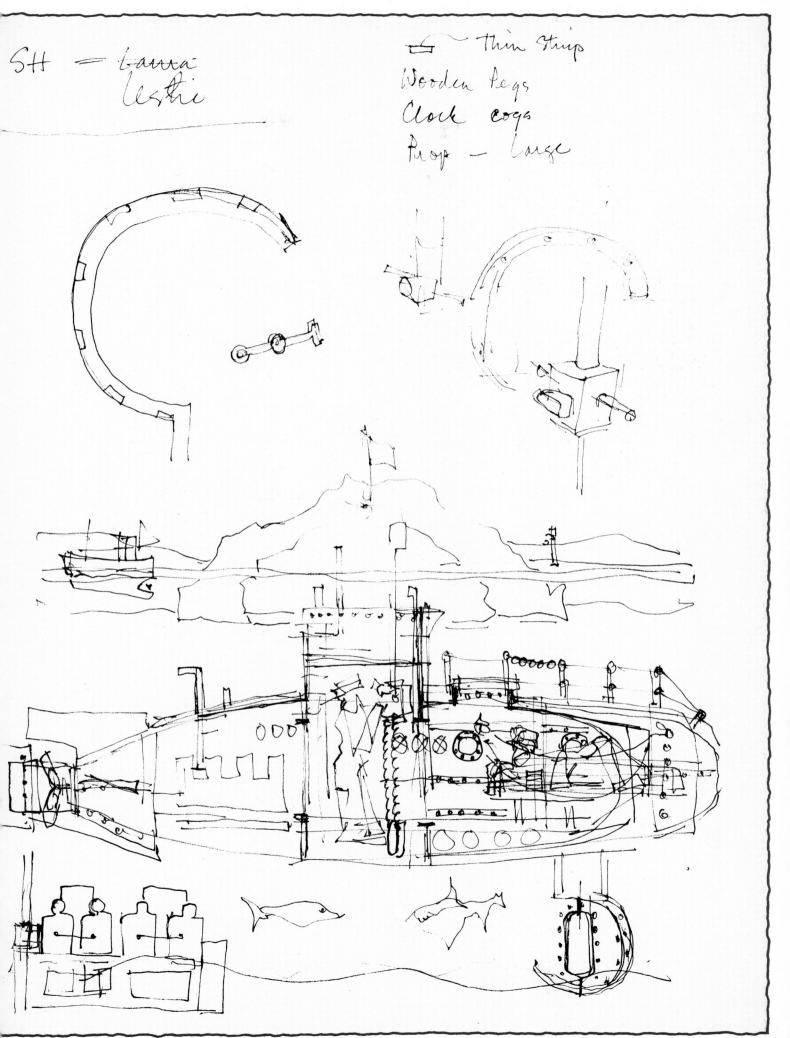

SH = Larra
Lestie

Thin strip
Wooden Pegs
Clock cogs
Prop — large

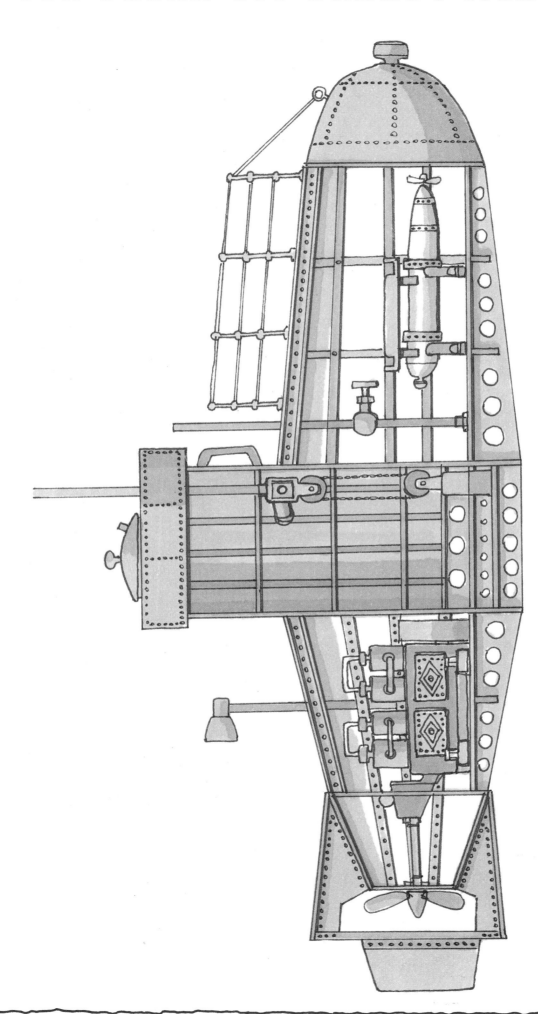

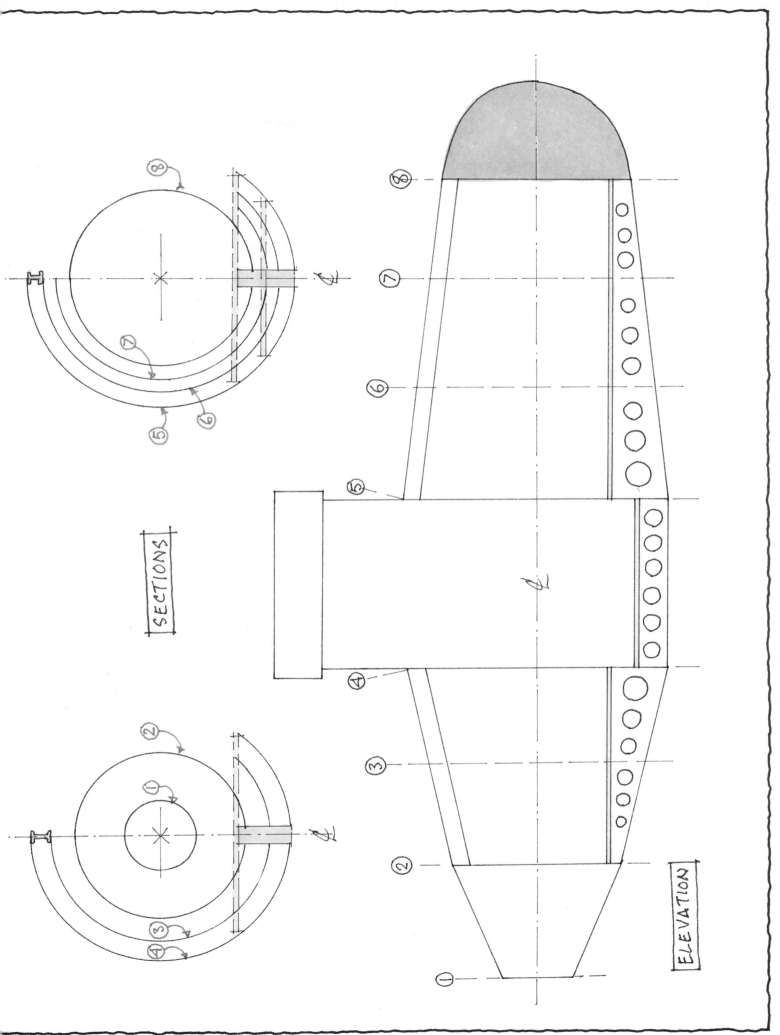

SECTIONS

ELEVATION

87

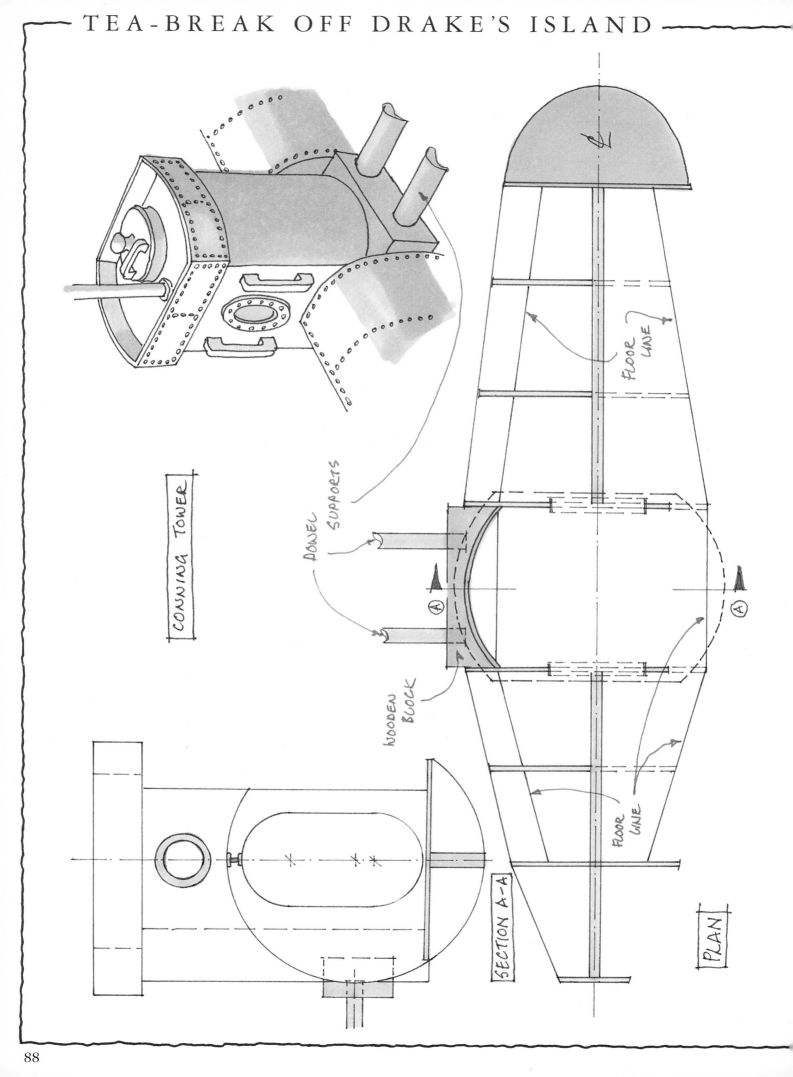

CONNING TOWER

DOWEL SUPPORTS

FLOOR LINE

WOODEN BLOCK

FLOOR LINE

SECTION A-A

A

A

PLAN

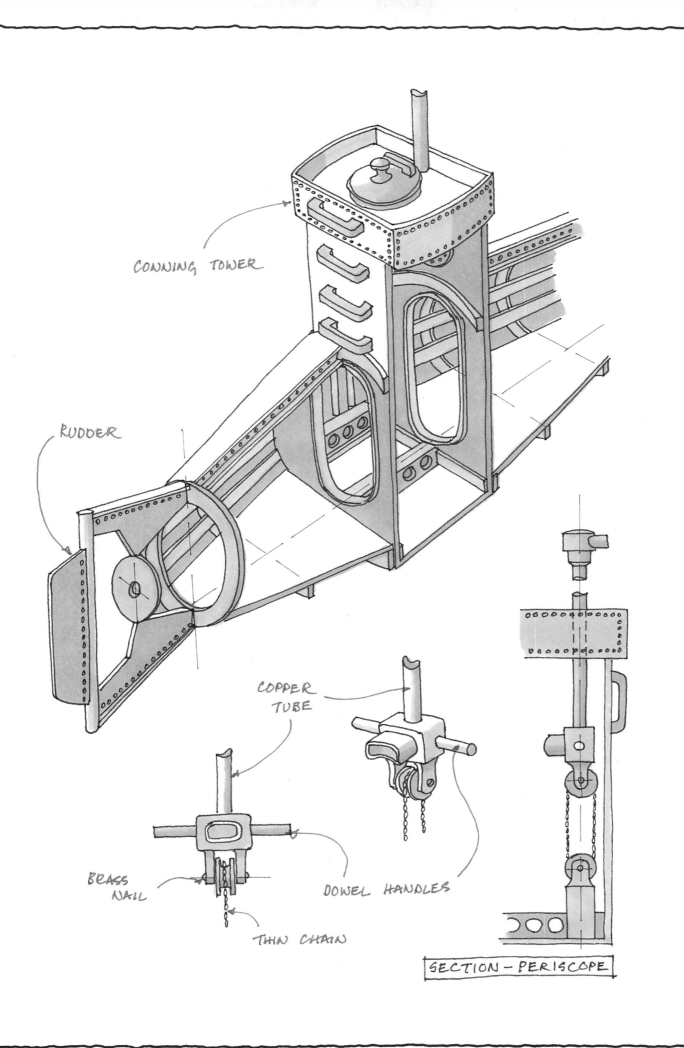

CONNING TOWER

RUDDER

COPPER TUBE

BRASS NAIL

DOWEL HANDLES

THIN CHAIN

SECTION - PERISCOPE

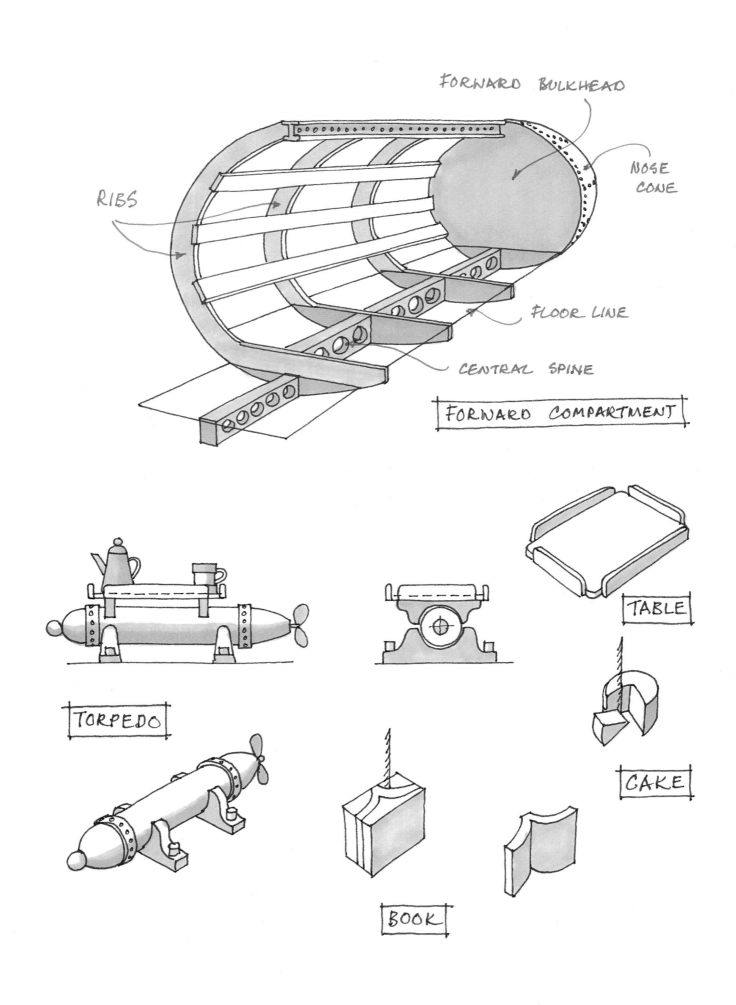

FORWARD BULKHEAD

NOSE CONE

RIBS

FLOOR LINE

CENTRAL SPINE

FORWARD COMPARTMENT

TORPEDO

BOOK

TABLE

CAKE

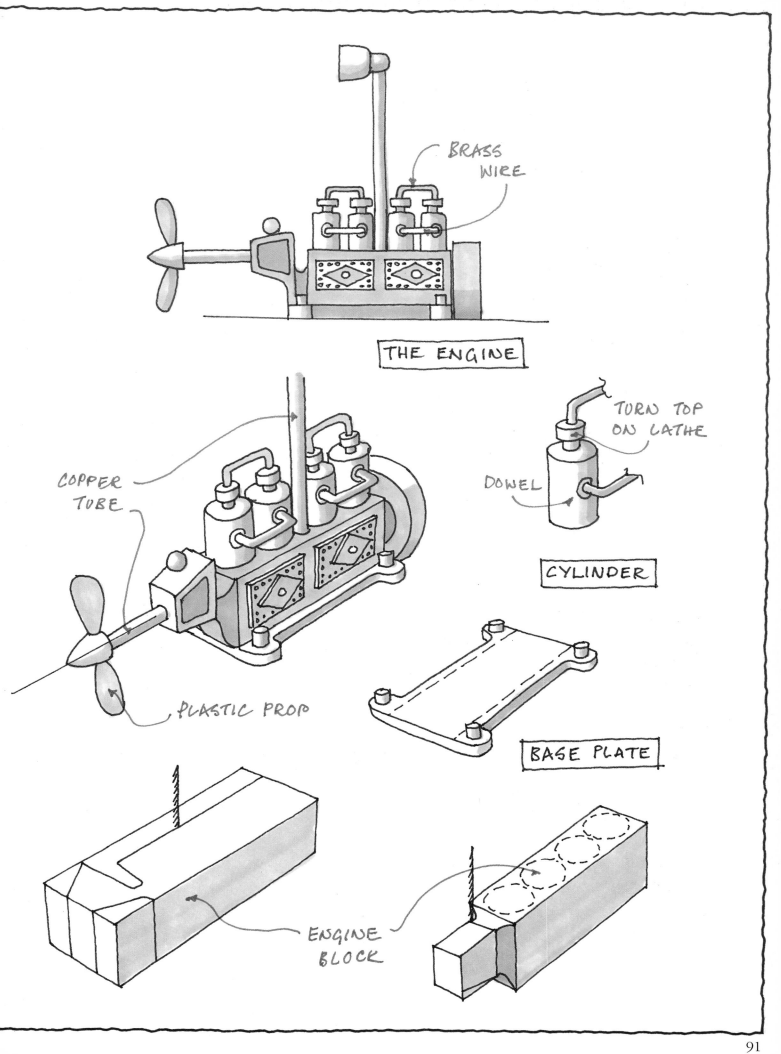

BRASS WIRE

THE ENGINE

TURN TOP ON LATHE

DOWEL

CYLINDER

COPPER TUBE

PLASTIC PROP

BASE PLATE

ENGINE BLOCK

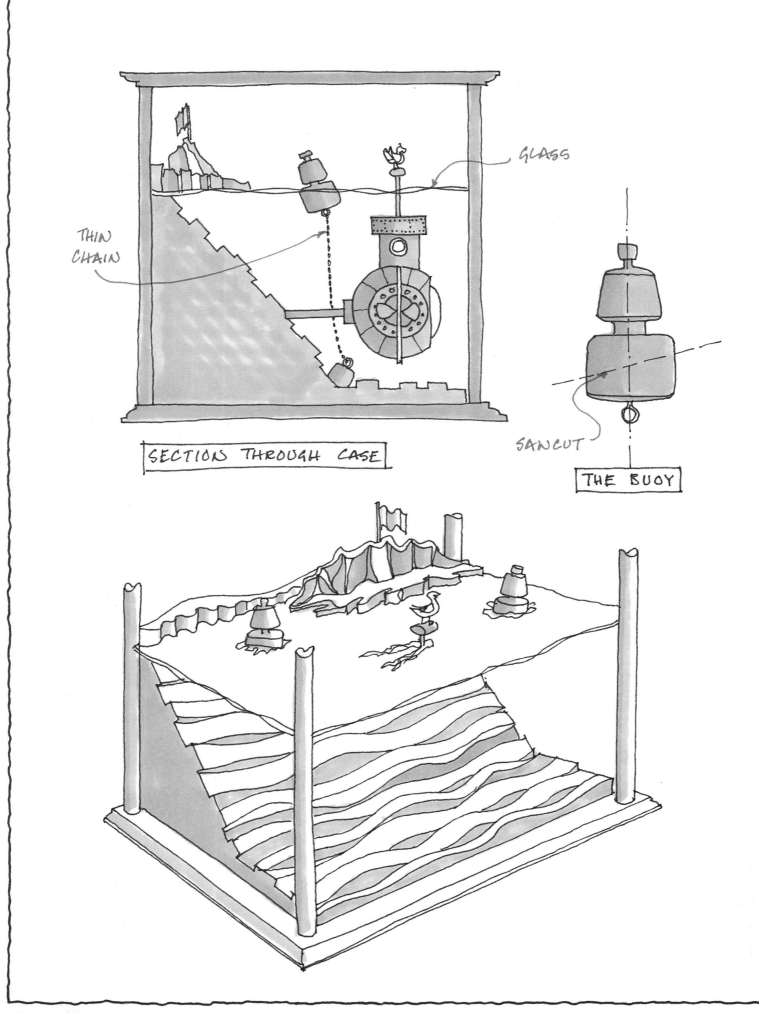

GLASS

THIN
CHAIN

SECTION THROUGH CASE

SAWCUT

THE BUOY

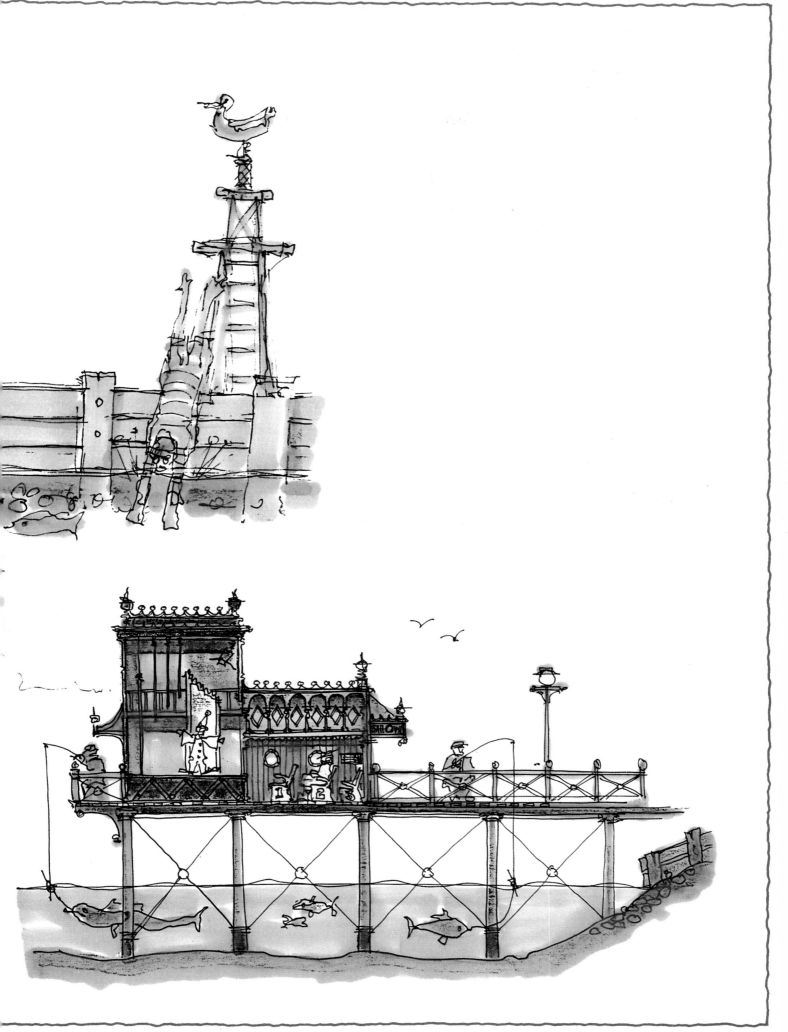

missing the
LAST
FERRY

■ ■ ■ ■ ■ ■ ■

This scene is based on an old-fashioned transporter which still operates at Bigbury Bay in Devon, taking passengers from Bigbury-on-Sea across the causeway to the popular Pilchard Inn on Burgh Island. The only difference is that the one here runs on railway lines, rather than balloon tyres. Too late leaving the Pilchard, our hero has missed the last ferry. What now?

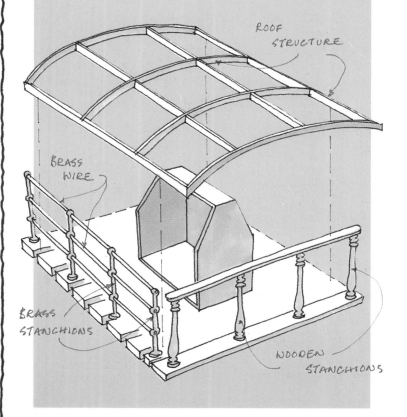

ROOF
STRUCTURE

BRASS
WIRE

BRASS
STANCHIONS

WOODEN
STANCHIONS

Guidelines for buying materials are given on page 10. All plans, elevations and templates are drawn to full size so that they can be traced directly off the page. Read through the instructions before starting and gather together all the materials you need. Remember it is easier to paint items before gluing them together. Make the glass case as described on page 48.

DIMENSIONS OF THE GLASS CASE
depth 10in (25cm), width 18in (45cm), height 13in (33cm).

1 Cut the main support joists, using the elevations for dimensions, and construct the base platform gluing small planks of wood to the joists. Leave a small gap between each.

2 The engine, similar to that in previous projects, is made and then fitted into its box and positioned in the centre of the platform.

3 The brass stanchions, available from good model shops, are fitted next. Use brass wire for the railings. Fit the wooden stanchions at the front and rear of the platform.

4 Construct the roof by covering the sub-frame, shown in the diagram (page 102), with thin plywood and then fit it on dowel supports above the platform.

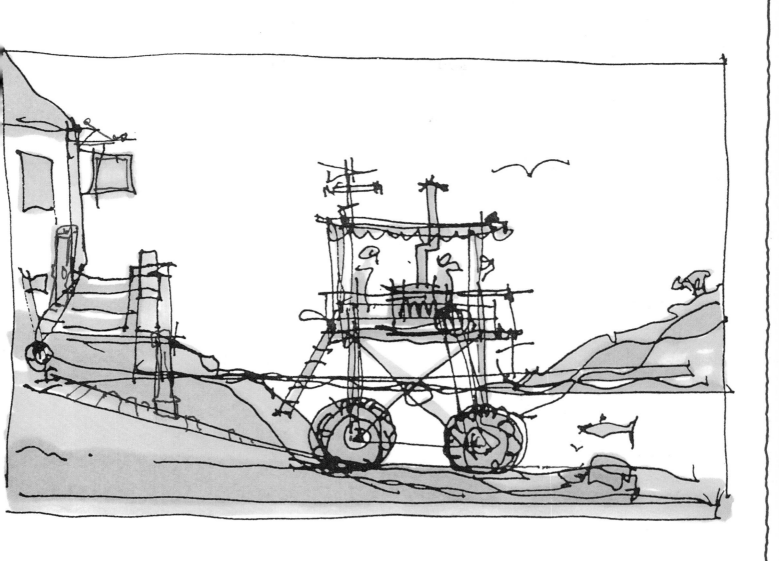

5 Use dowel, brass wire and map pins to make the handbrake and speed control and fit these in place on the platform.

6 Make the sea bed following the pattern on page 17 and glue it to a baseboard.

7 Cut out the wheel supports, as shown, using scraps of timber. Cut them in half before fitting to the underside of the platform. The lower half is positioned under the glass water's surface, directly below the upper half. The wheels and the railway line can be purchased from a model shop. The railway lines are supported on the sea bed by wooden sleepers.

8 Make the step ladder (see page 43) and cut this in half at an angle, the lower half is fitted below the water.

9 The Pilchard Inn and steps are cut out from thick ply and glued together, then painted and fixed to the glass water's surface with car body filler. Now the glass case can be assembled.

10 The seagulls on the roof of the transporter and the fish under the water are made with scraps of wood and fixed to the backboard with piano wire. Patterns for the life buoy, the captain and the passenger can be found in previous projects.

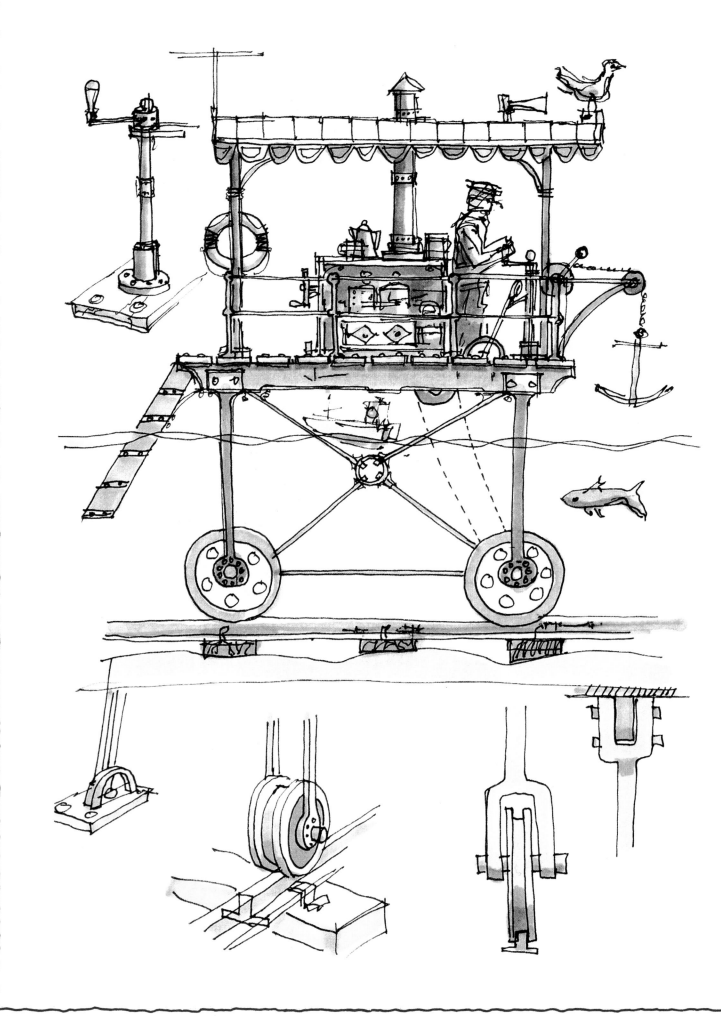

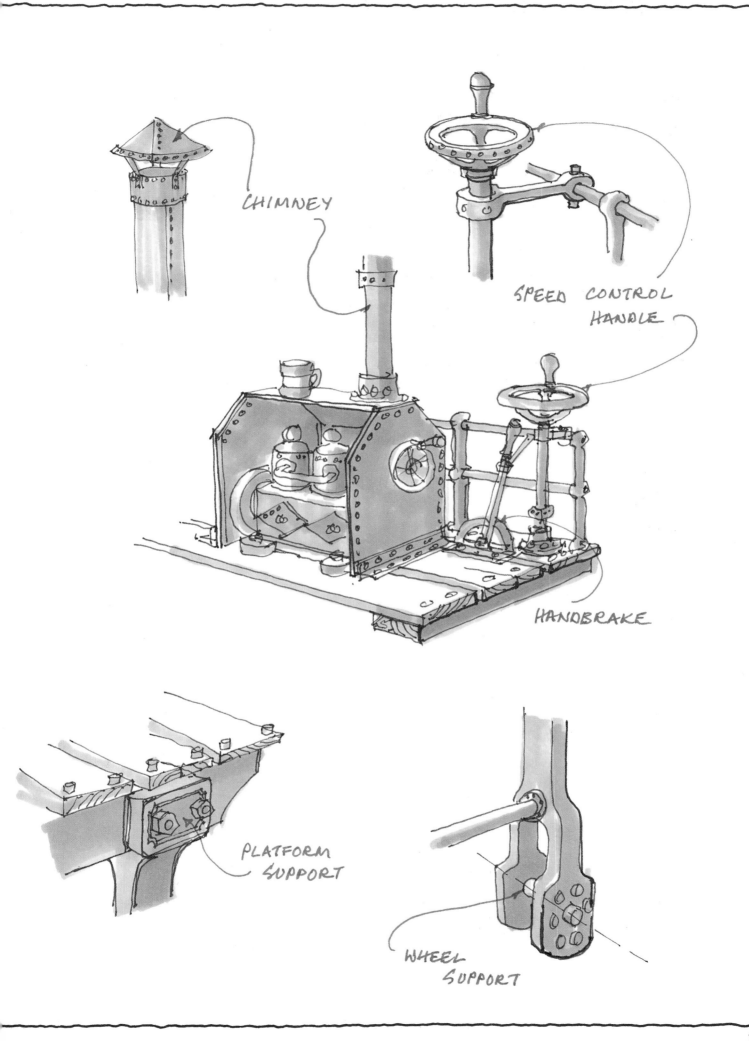

CHIMNEY

SPEED CONTROL
HANDLE

HANDBRAKE

PLATFORM
SUPPORT

WHEEL
SUPPORT

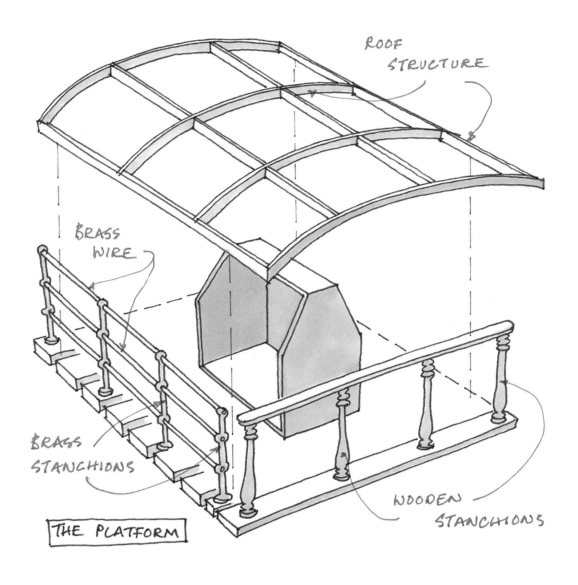

ROOF
STRUCTURE

BRASS
WIRE

BRASS
STANCHIONS

WOODEN
STANCHIONS

THE PLATFORM

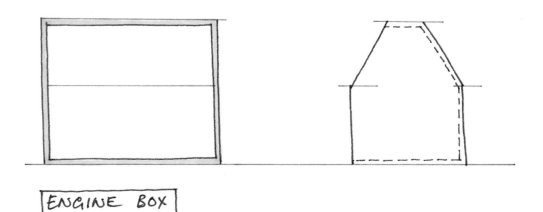

ENGINE BOX

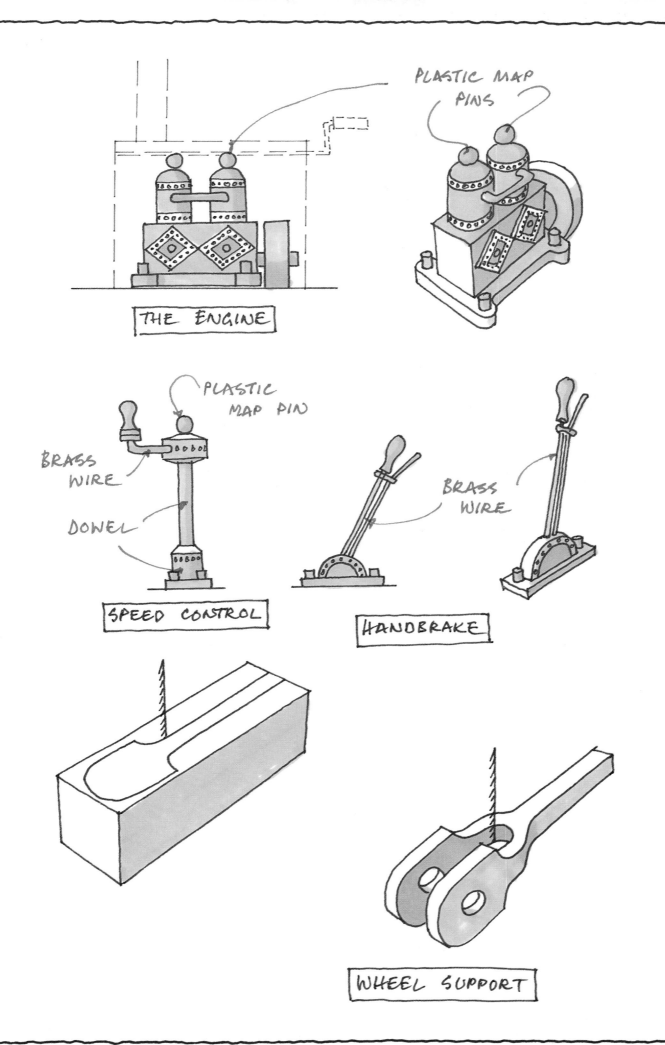

PLASTIC MAP
PINS

THE ENGINE

PLASTIC MAP PINS

PLASTIC
MAP PIN

BRASS
WIRE

DOWEL

SPEED CONTROL

BRASS
WIRE

HANDBRAKE

WHEEL SUPPORT

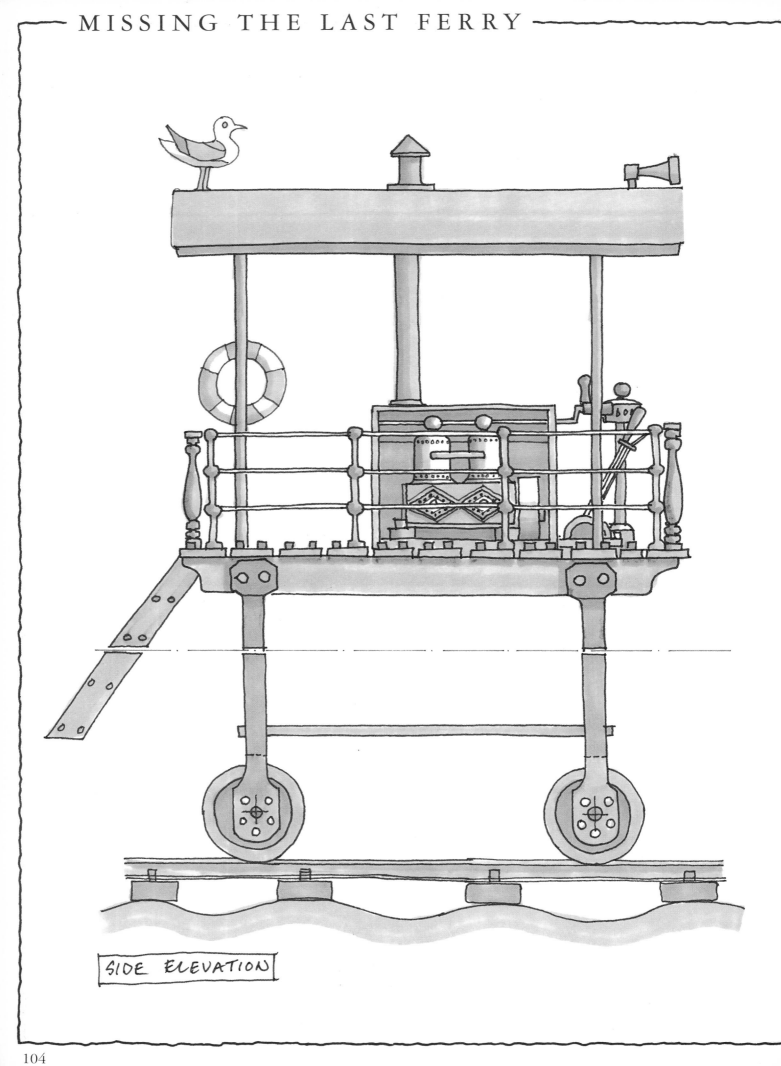

SIDE ELEVATION

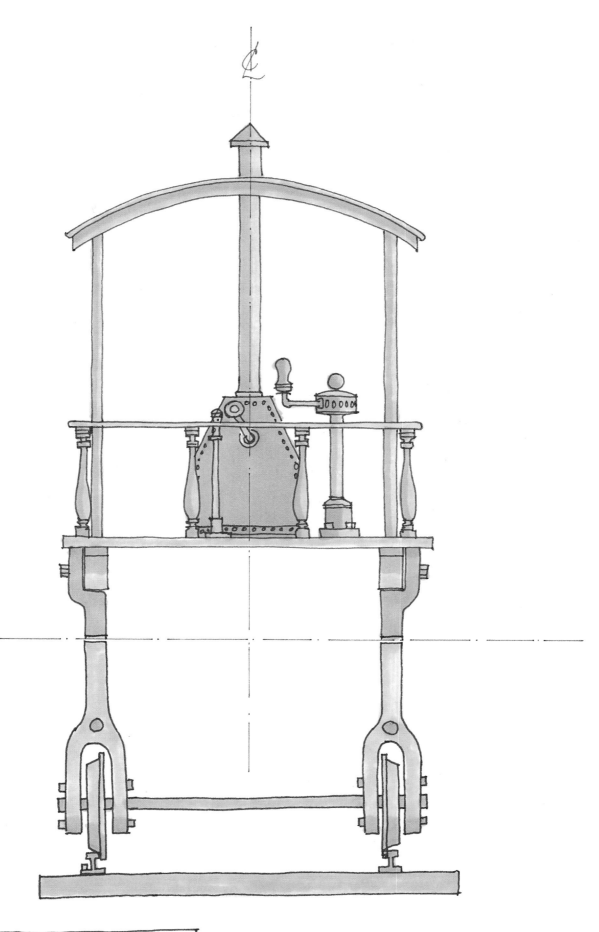

FRONT ELEVATION

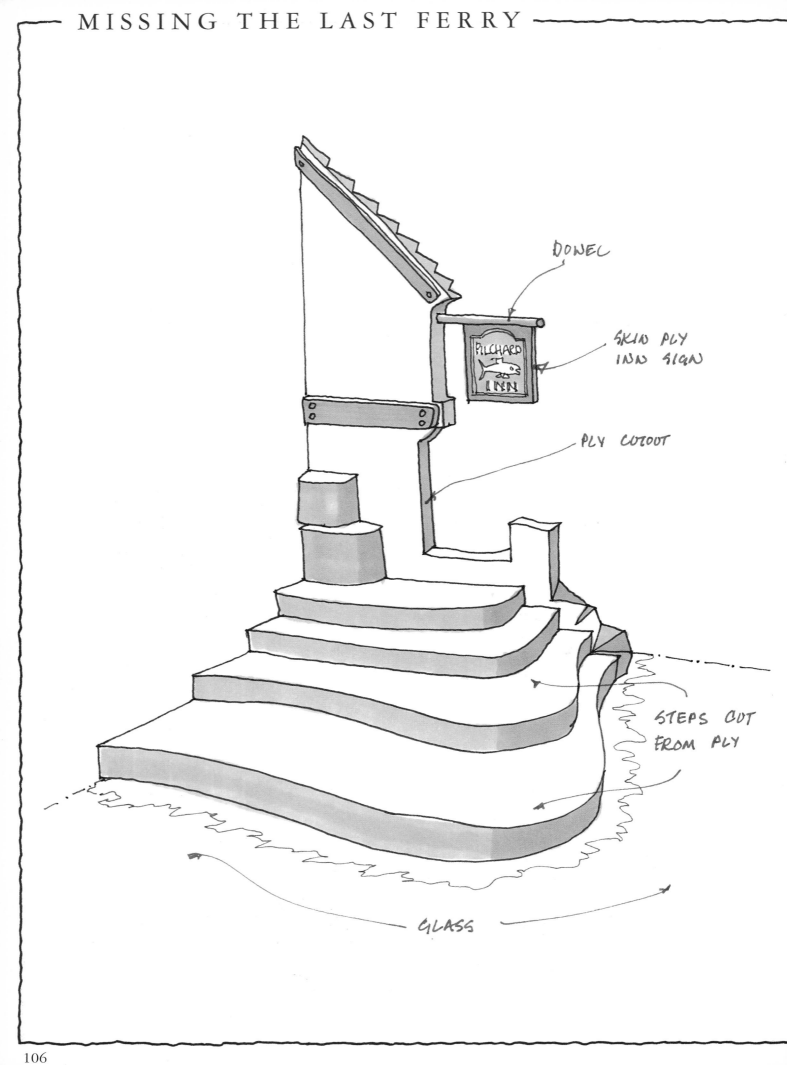

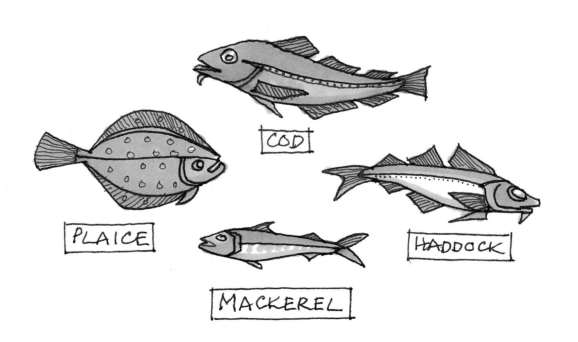

COD

PLAICE

MACKEREL

HADDOCK

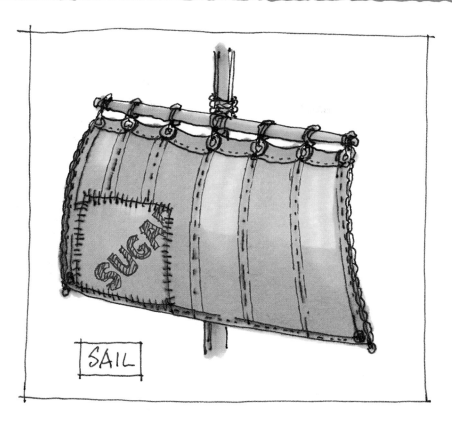

SAIL

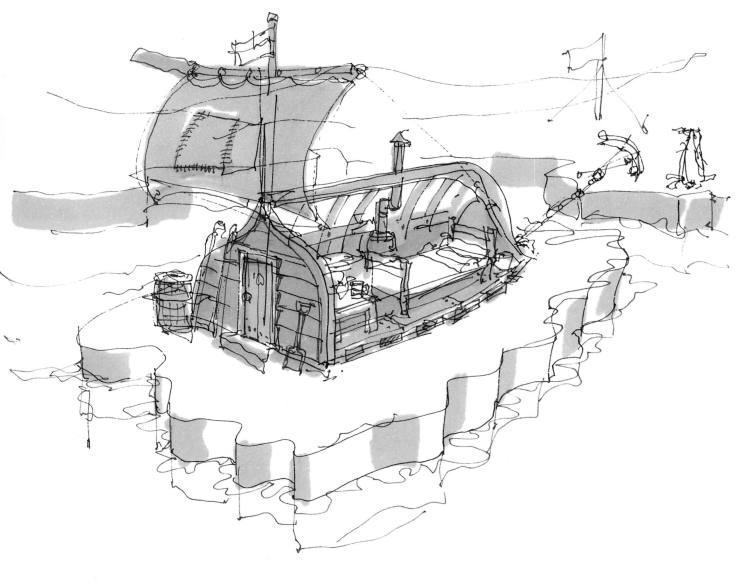

hoping for a
BIG
CATCH

A bright summer sky is the background to a man on his fishing boat. He has cast his net wide and deep to the sea bed, among the fish, weed and passing marine creatures. The fisherman, holding a mug of hot tea, is looking out from his boat in hopeful anticipation of a big catch. Most of the elements in this scene have already been used in other projects. This shows how versatile the designs can be.

Guidelines for buying materials are given on page 10. All plans, elevations and templates are drawn to full size so that they can be traced directly off the page. Read through the instructions before starting and gather together all the materials you need. Remember it is easier to paint items before gluing them together. Make the glass case as described on page 48.

DIMENSIONS OF THE GLASS CASE
depth 10in (25cm), width 18in (45cm), height 13in (33cm).

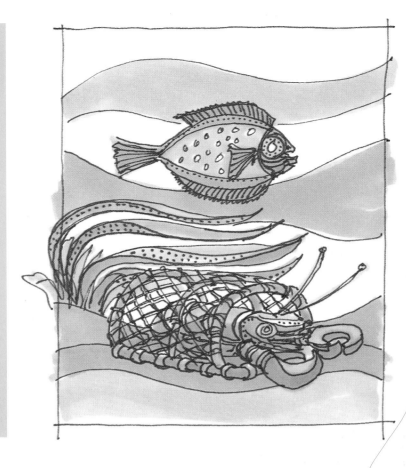

1 Make the hull from a block of 3 x 2in (75 x 50mm) timber using a bandsaw. Cut the rake on the deck first then turn the block over and cut the hull shape. Turn it back again and cut a slice off the top to form the gunwale. Cut its centre out and glue it back to the hull. Sand the hull into shape and cut it in half on a slope as shown.

2 Make the wheel house using the templates in *A Very Poor Catch* (page 42) for guidance. The only difference is that this time all four sides are used.

3 The deck winch is also based on that in a *A Very Poor Catch* (page 43) but is a slightly more sophisticated version.

4 All the remaining elements – the sea bed, fish, sea weed, serpent, marker buoys and the fisherman – are similar to those found in previous projects. The lobster, sitting in its pot is a variation on the crab.

5 Make the net from aluminium mesh bent to shape. The floats on the top edge are wooden beads with a slit cut to the centre.

ELEVATION

PLAN

THE CREW

WHEELHOUSE SKETCH

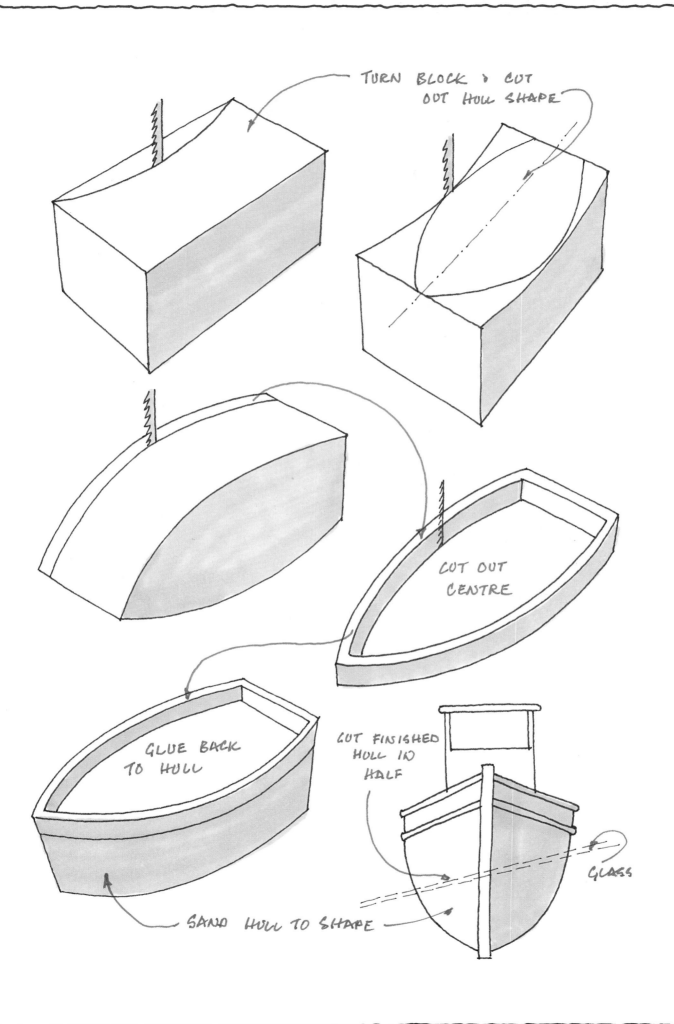

TURN BLOCK & CUT
OUT HULL SHAPE

CUT OUT
CENTRE

GLUE BACK
TO HULL

CUT FINISHED
HULL IN
HALF

GLASS

SAND HULL TO SHAPE

FLYING BOAT OVER EGYPT

INDEX

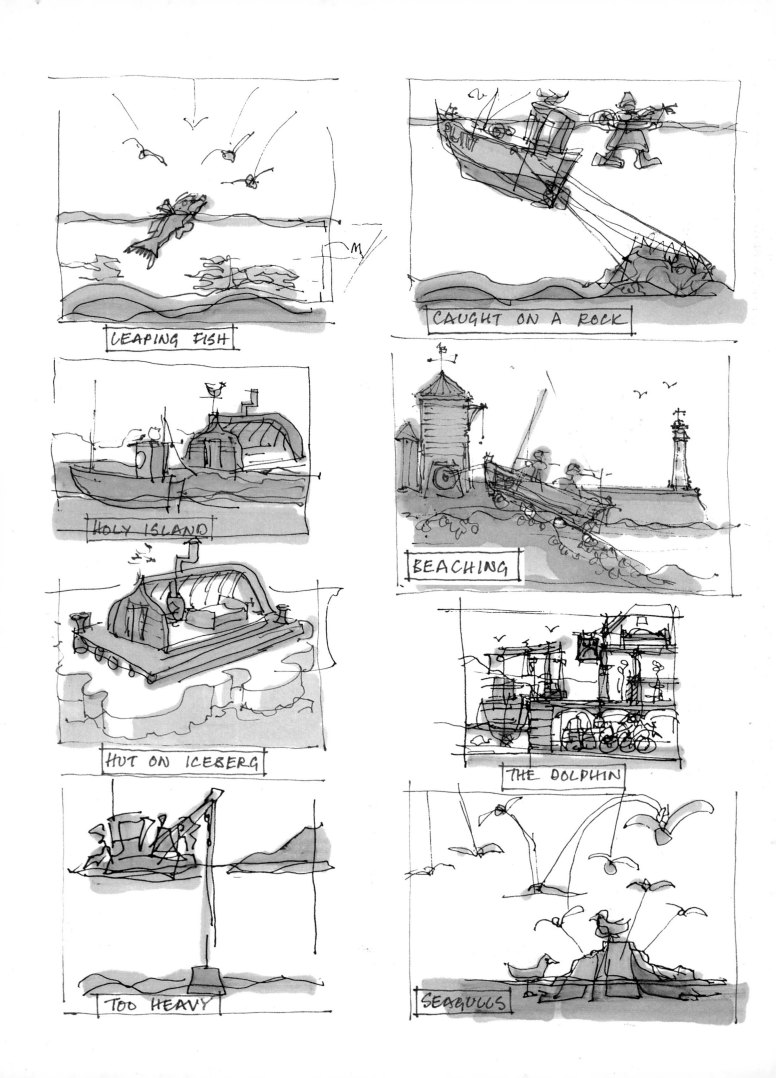

LEAPING FISH

CAUGHT ON A ROCK

HOLY ISLAND

BEACHING

HUT ON ICEBERG

THE DOLPHIN

TOO HEAVY

SEAGULLS